# BEING SUCCESSFUL WHILE LYING ON THE COUCH! REALLY?

*How to beat procrastination, develop confidence and take massive actions to achieve what you want in life.*

**WISDOM PRIMUS**

Copyright © 2017 Wisdom Primus

ALL RIGHTS RESERVED

No part of this book may be reproduced or transmitted in any form or by any means, electronic or mechanical, including photocopying, recording, or by any information storage or retrieval system, without written permission from the author.

**Disclaimer**

The author has made every effort to ensure the accuracy of the information within this book was correct at time of publication. The author does not assume and hereby disclaims any liability to any party for any loss, damage, or disruption caused by errors or omissions, whether such errors or omissions result from accident, negligence or any other cause.

ISBN-10: 1544069308

ISBN-13: 978-1544069302

*To my mother Marthe*
*who instilled in me the drive*
*to dream big and take massive actions.*

# Table of Contents

I DECLARE.................................................................................................

**Chapter 1: SUCCESS** .................................................................................1
    PERSONALITY ........................................................................................3
    INTEGRITY..............................................................................................4
    HONESTY ...............................................................................................5

**Chapter 2: WHERE ARE YOU GOING?** ......................................................8
    WHAT IS YOUR BELIEF? ......................................................................11
    WHAT DO YOU DESIRE?......................................................................14
    FOCUS ON THE GOALS AND VISION ..................................................15

**Chapter 3: START WITH "WHY"** ..............................................................24
    DECIDE WHAT YOU WANT..................................................................26
    DECIDE TO TAKE ACTION NOW .........................................................28
    PURSUE EXCELLENCE .........................................................................31
    DON'T WAIT TILL SOMEDAY ..............................................................32

**Chapter 4: PAY THE PRICE**......................................................................37
    GIVE TO RECEIVE ................................................................................48
    DARE TO DREAM AND DREAM BIG.....................................................50
    IT'S ALL ABOUT YOUR ATTITUDE .......................................................55
    POSITIVE MENTAL ATTITUDE.............................................................57

**Chapter 5: WHAT ARE YOU AFRAID OF?**................................................60
    IT IS NOT TOO LATE ...........................................................................65
    WHAT MOTIVATES YOU?....................................................................67
    DOES YOUR SUCCESS DEPEND UPON CHANGE? ...............................69

**Chapter 6: FORGIVE AND LET GO** ..........................................................73
    CLEAR YOUR MIND SLATE..................................................................77

**Chapter 7: YOUR SUCCESS STRATEGIES** ................................................81
    I-GETTING THE KNOWLEDGE .............................................................81
    II-DEVELOPING A STRATEGY TO IMPLEMENT YOUR PRIORITIES .....82

- III- TAKING MASSIVE ACTIONS ............................................................. 85
- IV – GETTING THE RESULTS ................................................................. 88
- V - IMMERSION .................................................................................. 89

## Chapter 8: IDENTIFYING YOUR HURDLES ............................................. 93
- LAZINESS ........................................................................................... 99
- PROCRASTINATION ........................................................................... 102
- IT IS NOT ME ................................................................................... 106
- DEVELOP A SENSE OF URGENCY ....................................................... 108

## Chapter 9: PAST, PRESENT, AND FUTURE ............................................ 113
- YOUR PAST ...................................................................................... 113
- YOUR PRESENT ................................................................................ 118
- YOUR FUTURE .................................................................................. 121
- WHAT IS YOUR "I AM"? .................................................................... 124
- THE POWER OF VISUALIZATION ........................................................ 128
- THE LAW OF ATTRACTION ................................................................ 132

## Chapter 10: MAKE CHOICES ................................................................ 135
- CHOOSE YOURSELF: LEARN AND GROW ............................................ 135
- CHOOSE YOUR FRIENDS ................................................................... 138
- CHOOSE TO BE GRITTY .................................................................... 139
- CHOOSE TO LIVE WITH GRATITUDE .................................................. 140
- CHOOSE RESILIENCE ........................................................................ 143
- CHOOSE TO LIVE BY FAITH .............................................................. 147
- CHOOSE SELF-DISCIPLINE ................................................................ 150
- CHOOSE TO DANCE WITH YOUR EXCUSES ....................................... 154
- CHOOSE TO BE HAPPY ..................................................................... 157
- CHOOSE YOUR LANGUAGE ............................................................... 159
- CHOOSE TO BE NICE ........................................................................ 162
- CHOOSE TO HAVE FUN .................................................................... 164
- CONCLUSION ................................................................................... 166

## I Declare

*I am a unique masterpiece*

*I am grateful and I make every day the most joyful day*

*I attract people with positive mental attitude*

*I persist and I don't give up no matter how hard it gets*

*I am a winner, passionate, dedicated to succeed*

*I feel my fears, embrace them and take chances*

*I choose my friends wisely; I give freely and wholeheartedly*

*I choose to be happy, and flow in abundance and grace*

*I seek possibilities everywhere even in adversity*

*I don't let my past become my future*

*I dream and think big and I create limitless possibilities*

*I learn from my mistakes and take accountability*

*I am humble, I don't react but rather respond*

*I'm willing to pay the price for my personal growth.*

*I am resilient, courageous and confident*

*Above all I love you and I believe in the Universe!*

**WISDOM PRIMUS**

*The Primus Method: _Serving With Passion_*

# Chapter 1

## SUCCESS

*"Success means doing the best we can with what we have. Success is the doing, not the getting; in the trying, not the triumph. Success is a personal standard, reaching for the highest that is in us, becoming all that we can be."* — Zig Ziglar

According to Collins Dictionary, success is the favorable outcome of something attempted the attainment of wealth, fame, etc.

How do you define success? How fulfilled are you or will you be when you achieve that which epitomizes your success?

What will it take you to become successful? Have you reflected on it while sitting on your couch, driving to work, walking in the park, or having a drink with friends?

Success for some people is the accumulation of wealth, whereas for others it may be health, happiness, and freedom. Martha Friedman said that success is "getting to do what you really want to do in your work life and in your love life, doing it very well and feeling good about yourself doing it."

Why do you want to be successful? What do you want to achieve in life that best depicts your success? Is it just to flaunt your affluence? What drives you to your success? Why?

The answers to these questions will illuminate your definition of success, the reason why you want to be successful, and how to attain your success.

Within this book, you will unravel the practical steps to turn your life toward what you want to achieve and take actions in congruence with your values.

Many years ago, I was working for a company that appointed me as the Operations Manager for one of the airlines they represented. I felt on top of the world. I was yearning for that position from the inception of working there. Here I am, all dressed up, looking dapper, shining from my forehead to my shoes, smiling from one ear to the other, walking gallantly and giving orders. Exciting, right?! Was I successful? Did I feel fulfilled? Don't ask me.

For some people, success comes in the feeling they have after achieving what may be substantial for them at a precise moment.

Success is not just limited to talents and skills; success requires time, doing the uncomfortable, working hard, and working smart with consistency and dedication. You can initiate an ideal life by thinking the way successful people do and by associating with other successful people. This comportment prepares you for success and creates the self-confidence needed to pounce on opportunities and form great relationships.

We need to examine ourselves and work on few aspects of our personality. We always tend to go after success by embracing many activities. In actuality, success is not always won by seeking after it. Often, success is something you attract by becoming more attractive to the marketplace depending on the skills and abilities you develop. Self-preparation is vital to success. A change in circumstances does not occur unless the change starts with you. An individual has the potential to be his/her greatest ally or main opponent. The decision to be whatever you aspire to become, starts within yourself.

By choosing to view yourself objectively during an emotional moment and understanding the emotion but not reacting emotionally, an individual can keep his or her eyes on the prize of a productive resolution. Let us explore how we can reach a healthy and lasting success.

# PERSONALITY

*"This above all: to thine own self be true, and it must follow, as the night the day, Thou canst not then be false to any man." — William Shakespeare*

Your self-image determines many aspects of your life. If your self-image is one of a risk taker, your actions will align with those of a risk taker. Perhaps that will not happen immediately, but it will eventually. If your self-image is that of a victim, most of your experiences will align with the concept of victimhood. The choice is yours. Ask yourself:

*Am I honest, reliable, and trustworthy?*

*Do I keep my promises?*

*Is there any congruence between what I say and what I do?*

Your words and thoughts will become the blueprints for your actions. It is necessary to live in synchrony and oneness.

Become a person of principle, integrity, character, and honesty. Look in the mirror. Who do you see? Yourself or a stranger? Your personality is an essential success trait. While looking in the mirror, ask yourself these questions: What is my name? Am I honest with myself? Do I have integrity with myself and others? Do I often do what I commit to? By reflecting on these questions, you are progressively on the path to discovering your real personality. Consequently, you will attract the right mastermind ally. If your personality is just a front and phony, people will reject you when they notice your defects.

Do not let vanity rescind your character. Develop a pleasing personality by honing your communication skills – verbal, written, and listening. Become an effective communicator. Understanding your personality will enable you to evaluate the people you meet. It will equip you to cope with them appropriately.

Most successful people share an extraordinary ability to interact and bond with others. They are quick to connect and to develop a rapport with people from a variety of backgrounds and beliefs. Your personality type and upbringing affect how oriented you are regarding the provision of solution. In addition, your personality can play a significant role in your ability to deal with and solve problems.

If your personality is not authentic, make a decision now to change and be genuine. You cannot portray a fake life and expect to influence yourself and others for a long period of time. Depending on the personality you embrace, you can expand to greatness or plunge in a downfall.

# INTEGRITY

*"The supreme quality for leadership is unquestionably integrity. Without it, no real success is possible, no matter whether it is on a section gang, a football field, in an army, or in an office."*

— *Dwight D. Eisenhower*

Integrity is the quality of being sincere, truthful and having high moral principles. Are you a person of integrity? Do you stick with your true feelings, values, and commitments? It is always easy to do right when you know what you value. It espouses universal principles for successful living and happiness.

Resolve in advance that you will rise to any challenge and never compromise your integrity for any reason. When our behavior is congruent with our blatant values, when ideals and practice match, we have integrity. There is no lasting success without integrity. You have to work and develop your character because it is the most vital piece of your success blueprints.

It requires dealing with every obstacle based on facts rather than assumptions. It includes accepting responsibility when things go wrong and focusing on the solution instead of the problem. Do you commit yourself to accountability and honesty?

## HONESTY

*"Honesty is the best policy in international relations, interpersonal relations, labor, business, education, family, and crime control because truth is the only thing that works and the only foundation on which lasting relations can build."* — Ramsey Clark

Sincerity, truthfulness, uprightness, and fairness are the qualities we need to develop. Back to the mirror, are you honest? Only you can answer that. You cannot expect to be successful based on dishonesty and treacherous behavior. Cultivate honesty and the law of attraction will magnetize like-minded people and situations. Honesty, integrity, and trust are three characteristics connected with one another. People of integrity gain other people's trust. Choosing to be a person of integrity has to be one of the most difficult choices a person will ever have to make. However, it is essential in our life. More than just doing the right thing, doing the right thing when no one else is watching is much more challenging. Also, think about the individuals who invoke the most admiration -whether they are living or not- and emulate the traits that make them so admirable.

If you lack integrity and honesty, people will find it very difficult to trust you. Now that you build your personality on Integrity and honesty, you are open to gaining people's confidence hence the walk towards success begins.

Have you reached your point of no return? Have you reached the level where you say 'I have enough?' Have you made the decision not to be broke again? Not to complain again? Not to look down on yourself again? Are you still too comfortable lying on your couch?

Most of the times we want to change our lifestyle. Nonetheless, we remain in the same condition because of inaction or not knowing exactly what to do. Have you ever caught yourself saying: 'I am going to eat that apple pie today because I will start working out tomorrow?' When the next day comes, nothing happens. No gym!

All changes begin the moment you are willing to accept the truth about yourself. You can change by using your free will and power of choice. If you want to go beyond your present place, you should be in motion by an appealing desire and enthusiasm of the future that awaits you right around the corner.

How successful do you want to be? What is the color of your success? What are you doing to accomplish that success?

There are many secrets to success, but the most important ones revolve around three areas:

- the purpose behind what you want out of life,

- decide what you are willing to sacrifice to get what you want,

- resolve to act.

# Chapter 2

## WHERE ARE YOU GOING?

*"People with goals succeed because they know where they are going."*
— *Earle Nightingale*

"Where are you going?" My mother asked me one Friday evening as I was walking out of the door.

"Really mother? I don't know. Why are you asking? I am a grown man, and I can go wherever I want and do whatever I want to do. I am 20 years old. What shall I be sitting here for?" I responded aggressively. "Do you want to know? Well, I am going to pick up a girl and some friends and head to Byblos Night Club. Do you expect me to sit at home doing nothing other than watching TV and hear my sisters argue all the time?

"C'mon mother, it's Friday, and you know quite well I go out on Fridays and Saturdays. I am doing very well at school, and you know it. Now is my time to party and kick it with my buddies 'Maman Chérie'. Can we talk about this another day? I gotta go Ma'am."

My mother answered, "Wisdom 'Mon Chéri [French word for my baby],' How long will you live this type of life? For the past three years, it has all been about parties, girls, and friends. Wisdom, how long will you continue on this path? I acknowledge that you have excellent grades; however, do they align with the lifestyle you are living now? I have been watching you going in and out for many years, in the same rut. Do you know that the rut can get so big that it will become a hole? Wisdom, you are my son. My beloved son, I love you dearly. I want the best for you. I am so scared to lose my son, Wisdom. I have been praying every day for all of you, your well-being. I will do everything I can to be there for you even after I die."

At these words, my mother started crying all the tears her body could make as she heavily dropped on the floor. My sisters ran outside to catch a glimpse of what was happening. They started screaming in panic and ran toward our mother.

My heart was beating fast; my entire body felt glued to the floor. I could not move; my cell phone fell on the ground, and I could not bend down to collect it. What is going on? Have I just caused the death of my mother? Is she breathing? I felt a big knot in my throat. I was speechless. One of my sisters charged toward me and slapped me. I felt no pain although my eyes were wide open. Am I experiencing my mother's death? May the Lord have mercy on my soul! Slowly I saw my mother's right foot move, then the left foot after which my sisters helped her get up and brought water for her to drink. After few sips, my mother motioned to them that she was fine, before turning to me.

"Wisdom, can I talk to you for a moment?" Mother asked while she gave the eye language to my sisters to leave us alone.

My body felt unglued and I ran to her, holding her in my arms I got on my knees: "I love you my Iron Mother. I love you with all my heart. I am sorry to put you through this. I apologize for talking to you that way. I, on no account will disrespect you ever again. I love you." I could not stop crying. She calmly responded, "Come sit next to me, Wisdom, and let's talk about few things. I understand you want to go out and visit your friends, go to the nightclub, roam around with girls. None of that is wrong. Enjoying this moment at your age is fine. However, will you do this for the rest of your life? What are your goals and vision?" She asked and kept quiet for few seconds. It seemed to me that she was silent for an hour.

She continued, "When I was in college I read a quote by Socrates: "The unexamined life is not worth living." Wisdom, it is important that you start thinking about your goals and set yourself on a course to achieve them. Go and bring a notepad. We will start now because as Confucius said, "Success depends on previous preparation.""

At first, a little voice in my head was urging me to go out as I planned and continued with my mother's talks later. As if she were reading my mind, my mother said, "I am sure the little voice is asking you not to pay any attention to me and go out, right? Wisdom, either you decide to go out or not; you are my baby boy, and I love you. Nevertheless, before I let you go, remember this: you have the choice to change your mind, do it now, and get your mind on the path to creating the possibilities for your future, or one day the reality will be right there in your face, but I will still love you. There is a gentleman who used to be a pastor and is a subject matter expert in leadership; I think his name is Maxwell. Do you know him?" My mother asked me.

"Yes, he is my best friend, and we hang out together at the library," I responded laughing. "I don't know him personally, but I have an idea who you are talking about: John C. Maxwell. Right?"

"Yes, exactly John Maxwell!" my mother exclaimed and continued, "Maxwell said, "You will never change your life until you change something you do daily. The secret to success is in your daily routine.""

The little voice disappeared from my mind instantly. Without wasting a second, I ran to my room to get a notebook and with excitement I said "I love you, mom. You are simply the best woman God has sent on this earth. I have a confession. I was going to see a lady I met two days ago. Nevertheless, I am sure that I have a lot to learn in order to be an awesome human being. Do you remember Kofi Annan from Ghana? He was the Secretary-General of the United Nations; he said, "Knowledge is power. Information is liberating. Education is the premise of progress, in every society, in every family."

My mother smiled, "Oh excuse me. Someone is catching up very fast. I am proud of you Champion. Everything I am about to tell you is crucial. It is like a drop of water in your mouth; it goes in all the cells of your body."

"You were born rich, very rich, and wealthy beyond measure. I am not talking about being rich in terms of money, but in terms of whatever you need to make your life enjoyable and focused as possible. The universe has deposited in you the necessary riches you need. But you have to awaken that possibility in you. You can set up any goal you want; you can dream to be whatever you desire. Yet, you cannot achieve anything if you do not believe in yourself. Now, let us start, open your notebook and write down 'Belief.'"

## WHAT IS YOUR BELIEF?

*"Some people say I have attitude - maybe I do… but I think you have to. You have to believe in yourself when no one else does - that makes you a winner right there."*

— *Venus Williams, Four-time Olympic Gold Medalist.*

Believe in yourself. It is solely about you. What you believe about your life will make it better or worse. Belief is your hidden power. Belief can become your greatest strength or your biggest weakness.

If you believe that you will ultimately win at an event, you have a hidden source of power in your performance. If you believe that you are going to lose, you are dragging a weight that will limit or destroy your endeavor.

**Believing differently will help you to behave differently**.

You can instantly reshape your belief about a problem or difficulty with this hidden power. For instance, if you are financially discouraged, considering another perspective will give you the drive to change your feelings. Author David Schwartz, in his book *The Magic of Thinking Big,* said, "Where success is concerned, people are not measured in inches or pounds, or college degrees, or family background. Parameter for measuring them is the size of their thinking. How big we think determines the size of our accomplishments." This correlation between belief and behavior will help you live more consistently on the journey to the life you want.

*Believe in* your abilities to sing when someone tells you that you don't sound right.

*Believe in* your abilities to smile when someone says that your teeth are missing.

*Believe in* your abilities to succeed at any cost, to make a way where there is no way.

*Believe in* yourself because the universe has granted you that power before you were born.

*Believe in* your abilities to cultivate and live a healthy life by taking care of your body.

*Believe in* your abilities to become successful and make a difference in the world.

*Believe in* your ability to rise up when you face obstacles.

Furthermore, you need to identify some habits you exhibit that are detrimental to your success. Most people have habits that they need to get rid of. Maybe they are too lazy, empty whiners, or have an insatiable appetite for sweets. They choose to stay in the same zone finding perfect phrases to justify their status. It has nothing to do with anyone other than you. Whatever your dreams and goals may be, you will find them hard to accomplish when your outer personality does not match your inner belief. You certainly know the habits you must eliminate. Next, set goals for yourself to scale down those areas which are harming you. Make a conscious decision to discard those habits internally by changing your beliefs and imprint your decision through action. Imprinting is where visualization and positive affirmations play a significant role.

Negative information will come and haunt you every second similar to the little voice you heard earlier, but do not yield to it. Instead, look for more reasons you can do something. Do not put some limitations on yourself. Expand your thoughts because you are more capable than you think. Your self-confidence depends upon the highest belief you have about yourself. Herb True said, "Many people succeed when others do not believe in them. But rarely does a person succeed when he does not believe in himself."

Do not let people make you believe that you are incapable of something. Do not allow their thinking process to take over and turn you into what you are not willing to be. Do not even worry about what people say about you, for you hold in your hands the power to create and design the life you want. Stay true to your core values, speak out about your beliefs and you will indeed overcome insecurities, and lead the way for others to change. Everyone has fundamental beliefs and principles that guide their actions; these principles are necessary to identify one's strengths. Develop and maintain a positive belief in yourself and your potentials. Furthermore, believe in others no matter how they may treat you, and progressively you will create an environment where you will attract more people with the same belief. Adversity will be looking for you in various forms, but you have to stay firm, steady, and keep growing your beliefs. It is essential in the attainment of your goals. Joel Osteen said this: "I believe that God has put gifts and talents and ability on the inside of every one of us. When you develop that, and you believe in yourself, and you believe that you're a person of influence and a person of purpose, I believe you can rise out of any situation."

"Have you taken all the notes? Does it make sense Wisdom?" My mother asked me.

"Oh yes, madam. It makes sense." I responded as I kept on writing.

"Another thing that's worth mentioning is the desire. You need to have the desire to succeed. Write it down," she said.

## WHAT DO YOU DESIRE?

*"To succeed, your desire for success should be greater than your fear of failure."* — *Bill Cosby*

Desire is a powerful inner force that pushes you to accomplish whatever you want. You must desire your goals to the extent where you can practically taste them.

"Assure yourself that you have to win, or perish in the attempt. Only by doing so, will you attain a burning desire to win. That is essential for success at anything. You must feel the importance, urge, and sensation of going after your goals, and when you reach that state of mind you become obsessed with it. It plays a major part in the mindset of success.

Wishing alone will not bring the success you want. You must desire success with a state of mind that becomes so vivid that you can see it everywhere. You become so determined to have it that you convince yourself you will have it, and you have already had it. It is the desire that separates people from mediocre accomplishment to the highest achievement. My son, do you have the desire to succeed and do whatever it takes?" My mother asked me.

"I do, but I get easily disheartened when confronted with obstacles. I promise you, I am going to work on my inner desire from today. You have my word, mother." I responded.

"As Shakti Gawain said, "You must have a true desire to have or create what you have chosen to visualize." Promise to yourself, not to me, since it is your life accomplishment and you owe it to yourself to find your inner desire. Make that promise to yourself. Now let's work on your goals." My mother said with a smile. I was so excited; for the first time, I started understanding what life is about and how to prepare my software before the hardware.

# FOCUS ON YOUR GOALS AND VISION

*"Setting goals is the first step in turning the invisible into the visible." — Anthony Robbins*

"Setting goals is the easiest, yet trickiest part of the process. By the way, I am proud of you for making this an urgent matter and getting on these tasks right away." My mother affirmed.

I smiled "Mom, why should I write my goals down? I know them by heart. It is not a big deal. For instance, I will be a millionaire and take care of you when you get older. I will build you a huge house with a swimming pool in it. When I get married, I will spoil my wife with anything she wants. I will be a rich businessman. Trust me mother; I've got it down pat."

I thought she was happy that I had figured everything out, but I was surprised when my mother looked at me with a curious smile, the type of smile that says, "Is that all you've got?"

Finally, my mother replied, "I like that Wisdom. You know your goals by heart as you said. Can we polish them a little bit? As far as I know, all you have just mentioned are noble, but instead of goals, they are only dreams. My son, your dreams are a fantasy if you do not write them down, channel them, and focus on them.

Your grandfather, my dad, used to sit down on the patio and tell us how big his dreams were, how he saw himself living. He told us about wanting to start a business where he would supply the hospitals with wheelchairs. Then, he would build more patients' rooms in hospitals. The list goes on. I was younger when he told us how great he wanted to be. We used to see ourselves in his dreams, living the life he was picturing. Your grandfather has already passed on, and none of his dreams has happened. Can you imagine how our life would be if he had reached them? Unfortunately, many people die and decay in the grave with their dreams for various reasons. I advise you to revisit your dreams and work on what you most want your life to be. I am not talking about today or tomorrow. I mean your short-term and long-term dreams and goals."

"This life will offer you many choices my son, just like a buffet restaurant where you can eat anything you want. Listen, Wisdom, when you walk in a buffet restaurant, you can start with a dessert, if you want. No one will direct you towards the array of trays; no one will bring you a menu.

Next time you go to a buffet restaurant, take the weight off your feet, and observe. Some people fill their plates to the point where they have leftovers. They let their eyes eat more than what their belly can contain. They stuff themselves to the point where they are unable to button up their pants. No matter how hungry you are, you cannot eat it all; and if you dare to eat too much, your stomach will not handle it. You can barely breathe. No one spoon-fed you. You did it to yourself. Do you eat because you are hungry and just want to fill the stomach, or is it because you crave a particular dish? Do you know your limits?

Before walking into that buffet restaurant, take the time to anticipate on what you desire to eat and how much. As soon as you enter the restaurant, you can make your choices; take the portion your belly can handle. Not only will you enjoy your meal, but you will also stop when your stomach is full. You will walk out satisfied and will be willing to come back another time.

Similar to the buffet restaurant, life offers you a diverse range of choices. Likewise, if you do not know what you want to be in your life, you will not know what you will do. Think and think fast, and set your goals by focusing on the different areas of your life:

- Social life
- Professional life
- Financial life
- Health and more

To start with, you need to identify the areas of your life where you want to have things accomplished. There is a difference between acting aimlessly and purposefully. We act aimlessly when we have no end in mind; but purposefully, when we have a target, a goal to reach.

Aristotle said, "An unplanned life is not worth examining." An unplanned life is when we do not know where we are trying to go or how to get there. It is a jumble, a mess. If you do not plan your life well, it cannot be lived well.

Is your current life a jumble, a mess?

Let's assume you desire to own a home. At first you may have an idea about how the house will look. You get the funds to purchase or build that house. You have defined your end in mind. Now you have to explore the ways to earn money, by either saving or borrowing. When you act this way, you act purposefully. It means that you are moving toward the goal you have in mind. Most of our actions cannot occur without thinking first. You have to think about the goals that you want to achieve and be certain of their consistency with your values. Then you plan how to achieve those goals.

Let us identify the types of thinking you need to develop.

*Practical thinking* will help you think about things you need to do, how to do it, and the outcome of your actions. It is the necessary thinking for purpose-driven action. Doing, starts when we put our practical thinking into practice to fulfill our aim.

*Productive thinking* is thinking about things to create. It is the 'know-how' that starts the wheel of action. In other words, you have ideas of the goal to accomplish and ideas about how to accomplish it. Productive thinking allows you to consider many ideas and find the reasons for choosing a certain way to pursue your goal. Until you begin to think and act on your goals, productive and practical thinking will appear unfruitful.

Do you know that you can turn your life appearing in a planned and resolute way? Get off your couch and out of your comfort zones.

Knowing how you are doing now is the starting point of the goal setting. While you are sitting on your couch or on your bed, at the kitchen table, in the park, take the time to wonder how satisfied you currently are with your life.

What are the areas of your life you want to improve?

Here are some examples.

*Personal goals*: These goals require self-development and actions that may become aware of by others or not, but will improve how you feel about yourself. In personal goals, you may decide to work on your habits, dress code, language, social behavior, smile, attitude, anger, emotional balance, happiness, faith, relationship, honesty, or integrity.

*Career goals*: You choose goals related to a job, vocation, either paid or not.

*Health goals*: You set goals related to your diet, fitness, weight loss, smoking, and drinking. Do you consider yourself fat or fit?

*Financial goals*: You identify goals related to money and wealth.

The list can include other goals as well. Pick each one carefully and do some extensive preparations to focus on those objectives.

Set a reasonable deadline for achieving the goals and list everything you can do to reach them. Organize the list in sequence and priority, but most importantly take massive action immediately. Do something to move toward the goal every day.

Do not work on your goals by relying solely on the capacity of retention of your brain. Use a notebook and write down the different areas of focus. Be time conscious when setting your goals. Do not set vague goals. When are you planning to be financial free? Give a precise date and time.

Ask yourself, 'Do I love myself?'

What made me love myself?

What is my passion?

What commemoration do I desire when I am no longer on this earth?

How can I reach those goals?

What are my available means?

What are 5 or 10 things I want 'to be'?

What are 5 or 10 things I want 'to do'?

What are 5 or 10 things that I want 'to possess'?

What are 10 goals that I must accomplish in a year?

Take the time and answer those questions according to each area you have written down.

Be very precise and targeted while answering these questions.

Les Brown always says that if you treat your life casually, you will end up as a casualty. Living with purpose and anticipation will grant you power over any challenges and obstacles you may encounter.

You cannot just wake up in the morning with no clear vision of how you want to make your day. It is easy to say, "I will go with the flow.' What if that flow contradicts your values? What if that flow is someone else's goal? What are your goals? Do not live a life of accommodation where someone else dictates your objectives and goals?

If you have difficulties identifying the ways you can excel, select three individuals you respect and admire the most and ask them, 'What do you think I am good at doing or where do you see me succeeding? How can you contribute to the realization of my goals?' Write their response and start working on the means to your end. Be mindful that the achievement of your goals will not happen unless you discipline yourself.

Write out a clear, concise statement about each category of goal, set the time limit for its acquisition, state what you intend to give in return for what you want, and describe clearly your plan to accomplish it. 'Something for nothing' is a misconception. Do not write some vague assertions such as I want to have a lot of money, I want the best job, and I want to look fit. It is merely insufficient to say those things. Instead, give all the precision, the date, the amount, the weight, the company you want to work for, and the position you want to hold. Be precise, bold and active.

Create a resolute plan for carrying out your desire, and begin immediately, whether you are ready or not to put this plan into action. Remember the best goals are those that stretch you, make you feel excited and uncomfortable. They are goals that require you to deliver higher levels of performance to achieve them.

Read your written statement aloud, twice daily - once before retiring at night and once after arising in the morning. You must believe you are already in possession of what you want.

If it seems impossible for you to see yourself in possession of what you want before you have it, here is where a burning desire comes to your aid. The fullest application of these steps calls for sufficient imagination. Those who have accumulated great success first dreamed, hoped, wished, desired, and planned before they become successful. "

"Unbelievable, mother how do you know all that? Where did you get all those information?" I asked my mother, looking at her baffled by the depth of the information she was sharing.

She stared at me and said, "**Growth requires putting one foot in front of the other and most importantly, putting one's foot in the step paved by someone you consider as a role model.**"

"Mrs. Lawson was my 7th-grade teacher and what a dedicated individual she was. There was no moment you would not see her reading a book, asking questions to her peers. I was so intrigued by her level of knowledge that I asked her one day why she liked to read so often. She said something I will never forget, "Marthe, if you want to live a great life, you have to prepare yourself for it. However, you need to get ahead of your present and feed your body from the neck up with the food that will make you the best at living a wonderful life. Resolve not to spend a day without reading or learning something new or asking good questions. That's how you'll grow."

She smiled and off she went. When I returned home, I asked your grandmother, my mother to buy me science, math and philosophy books because I was struggling in those subjects.

Enough of the talks; now go out with your friends," My mother ordered.

"Oh no, I have a lot to learn. I will party another day." I responded while I was ready to take more notes.

"It is all about balancing, take some time and have fun, my son, the important thing is to know your highest priorities and act upon them. Go and enjoy the night with your friends. It is 10 PM. I am going to check on your sisters. Tomorrow we will continue the conversation and the following steps." Mom responded.

My excitement to go to the club had completely disappeared. I sat there quietly, took off my shoes, and perused through my notes. I looked at the clock; it was 1:40 AM; I was restless. I went to wake mom up so we could continue the conversation, but she was sound asleep.

I started reading the Bible until I fell asleep.

I jumped out of my bed and looked at the clock. It was 6:20 AM. I got ready and went in the living room waiting for my mother to wake up. I craved more information.

"Good morning sir. I see someone is ready to learn more. Prior to getting into anything else, have you done all your chores today?" My mother asked.

Before I could open my mouth to answer, my sister Viviane responded, "Maman, what did you do to him? I can't remember the last time Wisdom woke up so early, did the dishes, dusted the furniture; he even did our chores. Did the Holy Spirit descend upon him or what? Praise the Lord! Hallelujah, thank you, Jesus!" we all burst out laughing.

# Chapter 3

## START WITH "WHY"

*"He who has a WHY to live for can bear almost any HOW." — Friedrich Nietzsche*

Follow your authentic purpose by asking WHY, the reason why you want to do what you decide to do. Why do you want to be successful in the areas you have chosen?

Indeed, you want to be successful, but what exactly does that success entail? What are you going to do with your success? What is the main purpose behind your will and wish to become successful? Why is it so important to you? Will you feel fulfilled?

It is necessary to determine the reason behind your drive to succeed. Whatever it maybe for you, you need to have a grasp of its deep meaning. Failure to know and understand why you want to achieve your goals, may lead to abandonment when you face the slightest challenge.

What does your life represent? It should never be something others have pushed on you. Instead, it should be the core of your personal brand.

What do you want your life to personify? How do you want to be remembered when you leave a room? The answer to these questions should help you find your motive for embarking on the trip to your dreams.

What kind of influence do you want to make with your life? Do you want to be remembered as a great leader, a humanitarian, or a writer, a successful business owner or a fitness coach?

Who inspires you? What makes them so extraordinary that you want to emulate them? What inspiration have you received from them?

If you pay close attention, you will notice that the people who inspire you may have values similar to yours. Their values are close enough that you could live in their skin. When was the last time you felt inspired? What made you feel that way? Exploring what or who brought this surge of energy out of you helps you think about what you value in people.

What are your natural abilities? What are your skills and talents? Discover them by examining your own life. The easiest way to find out is to ask your friends, family members and colleagues about the qualities they see in you. Make a quick survey list, "What are my top 5 abilities?" Distribute the list to your friends and collect the information. You will find out about your strengths.

You can also discover your strengths by taking the *Strength Finder Test 2.0* by Tom Rath. Alternatively, you can get more insight by reading *Now, Discover Your Strengths* by Marcus Buckingham and Donald O. Clifton. After you find out about your strengths, work on developing and mastering them.

It will help you create more opportunities and grow limitless potentials. You will better understand the ways to excel. Then, you can refine your strengths towards accomplishing proficiency and achieving your goals. You will be able to use your strengths continuously and passionately.

Is there a movie character you admire or once admired? Think about what you admired in him or her. You might admire Superman or Thor, for example; for more than their superhuman powers; it could be their ability to adapt to situations, help people, multitask, be super-efficient, and find love. Because they are fictional does not mean they cannot inspire you in some way.

# DECIDE WHAT YOU WANT

*"Decide what you want ... believe you can have it, believe you deserve"* — Rhonda Byrne, Author of The Secret

Be clear about what you want out of your life. If you drive on a foggy road, your visibility is constrained and can influence your speed. In your life, you will make little or no progress when you have no idea of where you are going. Without a destination in mind, your car cannot get you anywhere you desire and if you are constrained from seeing beyond the hood, you can wreck that vehicle. If you cannot see a direction for your life, you can destroy your prospects for a better future. When people are clear about where they want to be in life, they can take steps to reach their destination.

Successful people think about what they want and how to get it. Unsuccessful ones think and chatter about what they do not want most of the time. They are resolute on avoiding problems; hence, they never solve the ones that stand in their way to success.

Goals are the fuel in the furnace of achievement. Without a dream and the intense desire to change your life circumstances, you will remain stuck on your couch. Go ahead and be comfortable from morning until dawn. While you are sitting there, remember this, 'If you keep on doing what you've been doing, you will keep on getting what you've been getting.' It is your choice. Don't even think about blaming your parents, your dog, or your cat!

Choosing a goal for your life is important, but not paramount. Determining your direction and your pathway is as important as the goal you want to achieve. The journey is as important as the destination. Reaching your goal matters, but what is more enjoyable is what you become in this process. One goal leads to another goal. The obstacles, challenges, and fears you go through will shape you into a better person.

Decide what you want in life by assessing your current condition. Then, identify the areas you want to improve, reshape, and redesign. Circumvent being part of someone else's agenda. Create your own agenda and focus on the tasks ahead. It is feasible for you to live your dream. Choose your future and create it!

While on your couch, dream big since it is the starting point of your life design. Dream lofty dreams, and as you dream, so will you become. Your vision is the possibilities of what you will eventually become. Your ideal is the prophecy of what you will at last unveil.

Envision your future as you want it to be. Believe you will achieve it and move in that direction. Dream about things you want in your life as if you already have them. A vivid dream creates perspective. Abstain from futile sittings and dreams because an abstract vision is a mere fantasy.

If achieving the life of your dreams is important to you, start by writing your goals down:

- Write down everything you want to become in your life.
- Write down how you think you will achieve them.
- Write down what you think may prevent you from achieving.

The key to fulfilling any goal is to believe in an unlimited supply of potentials within you. Visualizing one's goals as already accomplished is one of the most powerful abilities accessible. The act of visualizing can turn positive ideas into positive realities. Based on the lifetime goals you have set; make a list of five to ten daily goals.

Get into the habit of seeing them through and move toward setting weekly, monthly, yearly goals.

When setting a goal, always articulate it in definite terms. Write a precise description of how success will look for you. Identify the specific actions required to reach the goals.

Know your goals, write them down, and carry them with you. They strengthen your will; they create a purposeful living, and they become the compass that guides you. When our dreams and goals are vivid, it becomes easier to know how to schedule and plan our lives.

Getting specific means identifying obstacles that could hinder the attainment of a goal.

The duration of your goals will dictate how often to assess your progress. Short-term goals require more frequent assessments than long term goals. You can measure your progress by evaluating success in each step toward your goal. As you do this, completion of each step accords a feeling of success and escalates motivation.

You need to find opportunities to act on a goal, and it requires some planning, significant effort and dedication. One way to seize the moment is to decide in advance why, how and what actions to take.

## DECIDE TO TAKE ACTION NOW

*Do the thing and you will get the energy to do the thing."*
*— Ralph Waldo Emerson.*

A decade ago, my manager asked me to join him in the conference room. Seeing his countenance, I gathered the items on my desk feeling certain this was the end of my employment. I had become a champion at tardiness. Although I woke up early enough to get ready for work, I was always late. My manager was unwilling to accommodate any more excuses.

I had all the alibis you can imagine to justify my tardiness. On a certain day, I even blamed it on having to wait few minutes for an elderly woman to cross the road. What? It is unbelievable I gave that alibi to my boss. Smart move, right? Stop it. Don't you laugh at me!

My manager unwavering in his decision for a moment retorted, "Sir, for the next 180 days, if you are one second late, don't bother coming through this door. Just return home and await the shipment of your items connoting that you are unqualified for this employment." As he spoke, he handed me the written notice.

I took a deep breath and walked to my desk. "Did he just mean six months without being late for the tardiness champion? No way! It is impossible!" I said to myself. I went home that evening and started looking for another job right away.

I called my best friend Serge Amela and told him about the written warning I received. He laughed at me and said, "Welcome to America, buddy. Do you think you can avoid being late at another job? Instead of running away like a jerk, face the music and figure out how you can be on time to work. Do you know what time management means?" He hung up before I could squeeze a word in. Even my best friend did not want to hear my excuses.

I fell flat on the bed while my mind was racing through the ridiculous excuses I had given in the past. Suddenly, my eyes caught a quote I wrote on a sticky-note: "If you change the way you look at things, the things you look at change." – Wayne Dyer. How can I change the way I look at being tardy? How can I turn this situation around and use it in my advantage? I do certainly know that I don't want to be labelled mister tardy forever. As I started working on a different way to handle the situation, I suddenly realized that I could make few changes. I decided to prepare the night beforehand. I chose my clothes, ironed them, and selected my shoes and socks; I put them in a corner before going to bed. Miracle! I had been showing up at work 20 minutes before 8:00 a.m. What a simple shift!

I had been hesitating when it came to picking out my clothes each morning. That was a cause of my tardiness. I developed my new habit and became excited to pick my clothes at night before bed. I achieved that success through setting up a goal and changing my habits. Some simple habits can either hold us from getting things done or allow us to be on top of our games.

What habits are preventing you from achieving your goals?

Whatever your dream or goal, you must change your habits and that implies giving up something. Synonymously, it means substituting one thing for another that is more important.

When achieving your goals, you will face disappointment, failure, pain, and defeat. Then you will discover many things about yourself, and you will realize the greatness that lies in you. You will become better, stronger, and more successful as you persevere toward your dreams. It usually takes one action to trigger a chain of events that lead to the goals. As Vince Lombardi Jr said "The man on top of the mountain didn't fall there." He climbed that mountain, he sweated, he felt pain, exhaustion, yet he kept on going till he reached that mountain's top.

Work with passion. Believe in yourself, and build your personality as the driving force to achieve your goals. No one will carry your load for you. Your closest friends may reject you. Nevertheless, you must rise to the challenge, toughen yourself, and build your momentum.

Your dreams are worthless, your plans are waste, and your goals are impossible if you do not act on them. The moment is **NOW**. How many times have you set a goal to lose 5 pounds? Yet, you are complacent about it. Until you get to a grocery store and see a person fit and well built like a stallion, you remember your goal to lose weight. However, as soon as you turn your cart in the cake isle, you fill it up with cheesecake, chocolate cookies, and more. Interesting, right? While you are picking the cookies, your eyes may stumble upon a person who is few pounds more than you are. Then, you give yourself a pat on the back. That little voice encourages you in your choices, "Thank God I am not as fat as that person over there. I still can nimble on few cookies at least." Oh well. The choice is yours.

## PURSUE EXCELLENCE

Master your skills. Develop a reputation for excellence at what you are doing. Your quality performance becomes an emblem of who you are.

Have you heard the statement, 'I hate my job but I am still there only because it helps me pay my bills?'

How do you expect a promotion when you say that you hate your job? You should consider changing your attitude before changing your job. You cannot bring values to your work place if you hate your job. If you stay at your job because it pays your bills, you need to wonder, "Am I just working for bills?" It is about time you change your thinking process.

Some people become professional fusspots, whining about every little difficulty they face. A few years ago, I worked with a lady who always nagged about how bad the company was and how she did not like her job. Her nickname became 'chirping bird' on the floor. She bragged about being self-sufficient and not needing to work.

One day as we were busy taking customer calls, we heard someone crying aloud in the corridor. That colleague just received her notice to vacate the job and return her badge. We were aghast to see her crying and pleading with the manager to give her one more chance. She articulated how much she loved the job, and she needed the money to take care of her family. Really? How can you expect to excel and be successful if you cannot add value to your job or whatever you do?

Let me give you some nuggets: if you hate your job, then quit, quit, and quit. Find a job that you will love to the point where you ask your manager to let you sleep in your cubicle. Do not wait until you lose something before acknowledging its value.

**If you are not satisfied with where you are in your life, stop bleating and do something about it.**

The personality you develop at your work is the same one that follows when you create your business. Give the best of yourself in anything you do, even at the job that you do not like.

Your actions determine your value in the market place. To multiply your value, you must multiply your strongest actions.

You will walk where failure fears to walk. You will work when failure seeks rest. Success will not wait. If you delay to take action now and achieve your goals, success will become another's.

It is amazing to hear people use the phrase, "I am going to try." Can you stop giving yourself a headache for a moment? You are lying to yourself when you say, "I will try...." Do you "try" to eat when you are hungry, or you eat until you are out of breath? Do you use the restroom when you need to go, or you just "try" to use it? I am not going to answer that for you.

# DON'T WAIT TILL SOMEDAY

*"Every moment waited is a moment wasted...."*

— David Deida, *The Way of The Superior Man*

Most times, people say, "I will do it, but it's not the right time. Right now, I have something else to do; maybe next week, another time, but not today."

This is what Brian Tracy calls "someday isle". It is a beautiful isle at the grocery store located somewhere over there. Someday isle is an isle you will never find.

Brian Tracy said in *No Excuses*. "Not only do we all want the same things, but we all know what we have to do to achieve them. In addition, we all intend to do those things... sometime. On the contrary, before we get started, we decide that we need to take a little vacation to a wonderful fantasy place called 'Someday Isle.' 'We say that 'Someday I'll read that book. Someday I will start that exercise program. Someday I will upgrade my skills and earn more money. Someday I will get my finances under control and get out of debt. Someday I will do all those things that I need to do to achieve all my goals. Someday."

Lots of people live on 'Someday isle' most of the time, thinking, dreaming and fantasizing about all the things they are going to do someday.

Could you imagine if Steve Jobs said, "Someday I will work on the iPhone." What if Thomas Edison said, "Someday I will make electricity a reality?" Picture Michael Jordan declaring, "Someday I will practice harder?" In each case, 'Someday Isle' would be far away from 'Just Do It right Now!'

To achieve your goals and succeed, you must do the things other successful people do.

Momodou Bah is a man I met many years ago, when we were working on a project. I have never come across anyone so diligent or having such a sense of integrity and honesty. I remembered visiting him one day in Saint Cloud, Minnesota. While we were eating, he jokingly asked me if I liked my job.

I answered, "Really, what job? It is just a job, nothing else. Some days, I find it hard to come to work. I am planning to start my own business where I will make so much money. I'll then quit this miserable job," I replied.

He laughed and said, "Brother, whether you like what you do or not, give it your all. Give the best of yourself. Then, find happiness and excitement whenever you are getting ready for work. Your productivity, promotion, and accomplishment depend upon that."

I froze, holding the fork in my hand as if I were practicing the mannequin challenge.

He continued, "Nature has simple laws. You cannot give a little and expect a lot. Life does not operate that way. Someone somewhere will give his last drop of sweat to get that job and excel. "Life was not designed to give us what we need. Life was designed to give us what we deserve" said Jim Rohn. If you have time to complain about something, you have the ability to do something about that problem. Doing something starts with us. You cannot change your situation unless you change yourself. There is greatness in you, and the only moment to bring it is NOW. Not tomorrow, not when you start your own business, but right now. This moment you are living in is the only one you can control. If you want to achieve your goals, stop complaining. Develop your abilities. Let your vision drive you. Do not let anyone distract you because of his or her own agenda. Have you heard of Aesop, the Greek fable writer?"

"Yes," I replied.

Here is one of his fables. 'There once was a speedy hare who bragged about how fast he could run. Tired of hearing him boast, the slow and steady tortoise challenged him to a race. All the animals in the forest gathered to watch.

Hare ran down the road and then paused to rest. He looked back at Slow and Steady Tortoise and cried, "How do you expect to win this race when you are walking along at your slow, slow pace?"

Hare stretched out beside the road and fell asleep, thinking, "There is plenty of time to relax."

Slow and steady the tortoise walked and walked. He never, ever stopped until he came to the finish line. The animals who were watching cheered so loudly for Tortoise that the Hare woke up. He stretched, yawned, and began to run again, but it was too late. Tortoise was over the line.

After that, Hare always reminded himself, 'Don't brag about your lightning pace, for Slow and Steady won the race!'

Momodou continued "How often have you seen talented and gifted people stuck in their rut while others reach their success through persistence, focus, and giving it all?

Do not rot in your complacency, but rather leave your rut and create a path where no one has been. Take action, do not wait for the ideal situation; there will be no appropriate time. There is no ideal moment. Today is your day of opportunity. The choice is yours."

# Chapter 4

## PAY THE PRICE

*"Opportunities lurk in difficult situations"*

— *Ralph De La Vega*

It all began on Christmas Eve, early in the morning after John departed to work. Marthe gathered her five children in the living room and informed them about her wish to go back to school to become a medical doctor.

A long silence ensued.

"Wow, Doctor Marthe Primus, that sounds good to me. I think you will make a lot of money and buy us many gifts. So, can I start attending the private school? I really like their uniforms. I told Dad, but he said he did not have that money to send us to rich people school." Viviane, Marthe's fourteen-year-old daughter said.

"Mom, it is a great idea for you to become a doctor, but aren't you too old to go back to school?" asked Marthe's thirteen-year-old daughter, Mireille. "By the way, is it true that every time you ask Dad for money, it always ends up in arguments? Dad always yells at you when it comes to money. Wait a minute— did you people fight last night over the Christmas gifts? I overheard him yelling again in your room. For the past months, you looked so sad, unhappy. I don't like his behavior."

Mireille was frantic.

"No Mimi, don't say that," Marthe interjected. "Your father is a wonderful man. He is a hardworking man who has always made us his top priority. We are just going through some financial difficulties, and I want to help. As we grow, our needs increase. Your father is the only breadwinner of the family, and he tends to overreact when I ask him for money. His reactions belittled my pride. I feel so useless at times."

I am tired of John's insults. When I ask your father to give me money I feel like a beggar, Marthe thought.

"How many years will it take for you to become a doctor?" Sylvie, her youngest daughter, asked. "What? Four years? That is a long time. I think you should reopen the porcelain store at a different location."

"Kids, I love you from the bottom of my heart. You are the best motivation I have. I am confident that we all deserve the best in this life. However, you need to understand that success does not fall from the sky as a ripe fruit falls from the tree. It requires diligence to discover your passion, decide to pursue it to create the opportunity.

"I am sure by now, you all can acknowledge our love for mango in this house," Marthe said, at the excitement of her children. "Well, listen carefully. The mango does not become this fruit overnight. Foremost, you need to find the right mango seed. There are many varieties, and you must choose the right seed for you. We can only get the seed at the market place, from a rotten mango or from a mango eaten by someone who has no use for the seed."

"Unbelievable mom, you talk like a farmer or my biology teacher. I guess a doctor can also become a farmer," Yvette said, laughing. Yvette became very composed and her countenance changed immediately when Marthe gave her 'the look.'

Marthe continued, "In order to make sure that the seed becomes a mango or mangoes, you have to wait for the right season to plant it. Do you think that seed turns out to be a mango fruit instantly? You wish, in the perfect world. Besides the right season, the seed needs the right amount of wind, sunshine, and water. If one of those elements is missing or is not proportionate to the need of the seed, the seed will die completely rotten. Few days later, and with the right amount of water, wind, sunshine, the seed will crack itself open and the bud will start sprouting tiny leaves." The kids were smiling with joy. Yvette shocked, asked her mother. "Mom, where did you learn that? That is too much. Do all the fruits we eat, go through the same process?"

"Yes indeed, my dear," Marthe responded with a coy smile. "That's not the end of it, children. As the bud is turning into a small tree, you have to water it and protect it against the animals, because they love to eat fresh plants. It tastes succulent to them. Therefore, you need to keep an eye, not even an eye, and all your eyes on the new plant to protect it, take care of it and watch over it until it grows to maturity. Soon, small mangoes will be popping out everywhere on your tree. You still have work to do. You need to prevent anyone from climbing the tree and plucking the unripe green mangoes. In a few months' time, the green mangoes will change their color to yellow with some reddish spots. What happens next, kids?" she asked.

Yvette exclaimed with both hands up and a big smile. "Celebration time, mother! We pluck them, clean them, and eat them piece by piece. However, this time we will not just throw the seeds away. We keep them and wait for the perfect season to plant them. Instead of one mango tree, we can have thousands of trees."

"Exactly," said Marthe. "At the beginning, you plant one single seed and have one big tree which produces many mangoes. From that single tree, we will get more seeds, preserve them, and grow more trees. We could easily feed a whole village with those mangoes by planting more seeds and patiently waiting for the right seasons. Do I make sense?" she asked, to the acquiescence of her kids.

"Wait a minute, mom," Sylvie broke in. "What's the connection with you becoming a doctor?"

Marthe nodded with smile. "It has a lot to do with it and life in general. Before I married your father, I was a nurse for many years. I put off my dream of becoming a medical doctor in order to stay home and be with you all the time. You are all grown up, and I think this is the right time for me to go back to my vocation and accomplish my dreams. I have always yearned to become a doctor, not just to make more money. I desire to help people and save lives. Some families do not have the same opportunities we have, so it is crucial to care for them and their children. Health is essential. If you are not healthy, you cannot enjoy anything regardless of all your properties, gold, money, clothes, and shoes. We have to accomplish what we desire on this earth. We must give and help others to make this earth a better place."

Tears ran down Marthe's cheeks as she reassured her kids that she was simply emotional because that passion was very dear to her heart.

"Kids, it is time to clean the house. We need to set few things up for Christmas celebration tonight. Do not share any word with your father. I will personally inform him but before you go, let's hold hands, and pray," Marthe said. They prayed and were thankful to the Almighty God.

Two weeks later, Marthe, courageously asked her husband John for a private conversation. "Oh no, not about money again, Marthe," John exclaimed.

With a smile, she reassured him.

"Not at all darling. Our kids are growing, so are the expenses to take care of them. Presently, we only have one source of income: yours and I want to help financially. The business was not as successful as I wanted, so I had to close the shop. A few years ago, I quit my job to take care of the children and submitted my personal interest to the family interest. However, they have grown up now, and I feel the urge to go back to work as a nurse. Ultimately, I want to take some classes and become a doctor."

"Become a... what? Going back to school?" John interjected. "How old are you now? Are you kidding me? At 39 years of age, you are thinking about going back to school to become a doctor? Who do you think will be paying for your classes? Don't make me laugh, my dear. There are many doctors already. Who told you that they need another doctor of your age?"

"For so long, I have been obedient to you. I quit my career, and then later, I closed the shop. It really irks me when vetoed any time I ask you for one cent. You become verbally abusive and irritated when I ask for money. I am not working; I am a stay-home mother; I feel you are a bit overwhelmed financially. John, I have always dreamed of becoming a doctor. I have always wanted to help people in need, especially in remote areas. It is not about money rather it is more about passion and dream. I am very confident that it will help our children, too. I am not too old to study. There is no age earmarked for study because each day emits a newness that brings along something new to learn. And learning equals growth. I do not want to fester forever without accomplishing my dreams. Yes, it will take few years, precisely four, but it is doable. I have the mental ability, and I can create the resources to help me get there. I have actually reached out to my former colleagues— nurses who are now doctors— and they are willing to plead my case with the board of directors at the hospital to pay for my courses. John, I will be going to school free of charge. They are even willing to talk to you and reassure you that it will not lay a financial burden on us. I have asked the board to guarantee a scholarship for at least one of our children. You know, Mireille is interested in the medical field and this is great opportunity for her to embrace that and become a professional with a free tuition." John got up pacing back and forth angrily.

Marthe continued. "There is a difference between a career and a vocation. To my understanding, a career is more about doing what brings the income in and helps pay some bills, whereas a vocation is doing what you really like to do even though it may not generate any income. However, I can assure you that most vocations bring more happiness and enjoyable financial profits than a job with steady income. I have a burning desire." She opened up her purse and took out an old diary completely worn out with time. "This notebook contains my life dreams, visions, and goals. My uncle gave it to me when I was in seventh grade and told me to keep it with me anywhere I go so that whenever I have an idea, I can write it down and pray, work till I achieve that. Look, on the first page I wrote this: 'I want to become a medical doctor and help people to be healthy and cure diseases.' I promise to go to school and become the first doctor in my family. Why are you doing this to me John, why do you want to hold me back? It is for my own good and the good of our family. Am I not a human being? Do I not have a voice to express my wishes? Am I not also the daughter of the Almighty God? Do you want me to settle my life just as being a stay-home mother? What will I do when you retire and when the kids move out?" She got on her knees at her husband's feet, sobbing, crying, and pleading. John moved his left foot, burst the door open, walked out to his car without uttering a word, and drove off.

Few minutes later, her oldest daughter, Yvette, opened her parents' door and walked in angrily.

"Mom, stop crying. You are our mother, and we fully support you. We were listening behind the door while you pleaded your case with Dad. Is it true that you wrote this in your diary in seventh grade?" Marthe nodded, starring at her tears wetting the floor. "You are going to become a medical doctor whether Dad wants it or not.

"Don't worry about us. Viviane and I will take care of our siblings. We are no longer children," Yvette assured. "School is out on Monday, so we will be with you when you go back to classes. Remember, you always tell us not to give up on ourselves, and during our troubles, we must aspire to turn it into a new possibility. On Monday, you will create your new future with new possibilities. *If God is for us, who can be against us?"*

"Pastor Yvette, preach, preach, preach," all the kids exclaimed. Marthe smiled, got up, and they held hands and prayed for strength.

The sun was setting on the horizon illuminating the sky with its last rays. Marthe was standing at the gate admiring the scene. Suddenly, the clouds darkened the sky, blocking the beautiful view of the sunset. She saw John's car pulling over. Her heartbeat as her eyes crossed the daring look of her husband.

"I need to talk to you now. Come here." John ordered. "It seems to me like you are determined to go back to school to become 'whatever' doctor you want to call yourself. I spoke with few of my friends and they felt that you are hiding something, maybe a lover, or maybe you want to show me that you can make more money than I do. Who knows? That decision of yours is not at all welcome. You either remain at home as married, or follow your dreams and be divorced. You are free to leave this house now or anytime, henceforth, you will move to the guest room. Additionally, I am taking the car from you. Your doctors can buy you another one."

"Thank you. I will do whatever it takes to become a medical doctor, help people and fulfill my vocation, and if being divorced is the consequence, then I am willing to pay the price. So, help me God," Marthe responded defiantly.

John got up and walked to the kids' room.

"Listen to me carefully. Your mother wants to go back to school to become a doctor. I do not believe it. I am sure she wants to have freedom to see other men. I do not even know whether you are really my kids. If you want to follow her with her so-called dreams, be my guest and go with her, but don't ever come and ask me for anything." He slammed the door and walked away.

Marthe called her brother Agos who came in and helped her carry few items. Her kids decided to follow her and they all left.

On the way to her brother's house, everybody was quiet. They could only hear the sound of the car engine. Many thoughts were going through Marthe's mind. How am I going to take care of my kids all by myself? Am I selfish thinking only about my goals and dreams instead of settling there and taking care of my kids? She wondered. She could hear the little voice in her saying. "Take a deep breath. Were you happy with your life? Do you want to be like those people who die without having the courage to face the odds, unleash their full potential, and reach their goals? Imagine the number of people you will touch with your new skills. This is the best opportunity for you to design your life and create new possibilities. Look into your kids' eyes. Do you see the past, the present, or a great future you can create for yourself to inspire them to create theirs? You have the power to choose your own destiny. Now is the time to challenge yourself and bring out the greatness that lies dormant in you. How long do you want to squash that thirst for your own success? How long, Marthe?

"You'd better wipe your tears now, lift your head up high, bump your chest, flex your muscles, and brace up for your fight to succeed. Remember that actions bring results. You already know your target and that is becoming a doctor to help people be healthy. The most exciting thing to do is begin a process with the end in mind. If you possess a bare land to build a house on, to begin with, you need to build that house in your mind, and then model it and start working on it piece by piece. The actualization of the first two steps becomes active by practicing effective self-management. Manage your life according to your priorities and needs, not according to your wants. Spend time doing what fits into your personal mission, identify the key roles that you take on in life, and make time for each of them. Hold on right there! Do not think negatively. Are you listening? I am talking to you Marthe."

"Imagine how your achievements will encourage your kids to dream big and better, to identify, and develop their goals. Imagine the impact it will have in their life. Have they not decided to follow and support you? Well, your move will also benefit them in the end since there is no turning back. You cannot achieve a future while walking backwards. There is no such a thing as 'backward future.' I don't think that even sounds compelling to you, does it? This is not going to be a quick and easy process, Marthe, but results will certainly ensue after applying those concepts. Now turn around and give the kids a reassuring smile. They need it."

Slowly, Marthe looked at her kids in the back seat and said. *"If God is for us, who can be against us?"*

They all repeated in chorus and laughed.

Marthe is my mother, my late mother.

I was 11 years old when it happened. Mom used to be vibrant, energetic, and bubbling. All my classmates and teachers loved her, because she always greeted everyone warmly, and encouraged all the students to do their hardest and to listen to the teachers.

The day she gathered us in the living room and informed us about going back to school to become a doctor, I did not understand much about what a doctor could do other than give me some painful shots when I was ill. However, I could see the sadness and the tears in her face. She had a wrinkled white shirt and a long skirt on, her hands on her chest and her hair unmade. She sat barefoot on the floor, confused and sad, yet determined. She cried and cried a lot. Her eyes were void of expression. It seemed like she was living a nightmare. She felt abandoned by the man she sacrificed her job and business for, the man who promised to go through thick and thin with her, the man who carried her and danced with her, the man she loved and called her husband, the father of their children. I felt so weak, useless, and angry. What could I do? I wanted to wait at the main gate for my father to come back, so I could tell him to honor my mother's request. I cried along with her. I felt a deep pain as if my heart was ready to spring out of my chest. The more I looked into my mother's eyes, the heavier I breathed. I loved my father, but I could not bear to see him hurt my mother this way. She is my mother, and she means the world to me. As I was staring at her tears drenching her cheeks, I scooted close to her and with my little hands I wiped her tears and said "mommy, I will protect you and I will take care of you."

My uncle was residing in a two-bedroom house. Our mother shared one room with two of my sisters, and I slept in the living room with the others. We did not have the full comfort of our father's house, yet we felt a heavy burden lifted from our heart. Mom was happier, and so were my sisters. At school, some friends noticed our mother's absence in the evening when she used to come and pick us up after classes. We walked one hour from school to Uncle Agos' house. It was fun walking with our friends, enjoying the view, and passing through some houses. I felt so delighted with our new life. Mother used to tell us, "What you have today may vanish tomorrow, but remember this; life goes on with little or nothing. Show your appreciation and gratitude to life, find the deep happiness in yourself, and smile while remembering that as long as we still breathe, we move."

During all three months that we stayed with our uncle, I had never heard our mother complain. She exuded a new confidence we had not seen before. Every morning, we held hands, prayed and embraced the day with gratitude and expectation. I could not understand why she used to ask for grace upon us. "Give us grace and help us discover new possibilities" she always said. Soon after moving in with our uncle, Mom went back to work in the evening while she attended school in the morning. My uncle was puzzled by her strong will, belief and determination to achieve her dreams.

"Be diligent and bring high value to yourself and whatever you do, then life will reward you," she told me one morning while she was getting ready for her classes. I did not understand what she meant until one day at sunset when she gathered us all in the living room, and silently, she started crying like never before. We were all surprised to see tears coming out of her pretty eyes.

---

*Life is a ride full of ups and downs, but never lose sight of your destination.*

---

Lifting her head up, our mother looked in our eyes and a smile shone through her tears as she announced that grace had fallen upon us.

"Kids, life remains a ride full of vicissitudes, but never lose sight of your destination. I had a meeting with the board of directors of the hospital, and they reviewed my school records...." she paused.

"What is next mother? Have you failed? Please talk to us!" Yvette asked as she put both hands on her head as if the world has fallen apart.

"Kids, age has nothing to do with school. Age cannot debar you from moving forward and doing what you decide to do. So many people, including my family members advised me to give up schooling and my dreams. Some friends even advised that I drop the impossibilities and embrace the reality. They gave me examples of others who tried but failed and urged me to simply work and make some money to take care of us. Nothing can stop you. Unless there is an enemy within, the enemy outside can do you no harm. The school has recommended that I skip few classes and become an assistant to the head doctor of the hospital. We have been given a doctor's residence, a five-bedroom house for as long as we desire and as long as I still work at the hospital and take classes." My sister Mireille screamed on top of her lungs.

"Patience," Mom said. "Mireille, you told me you wanted to embrace my career, the opportunity has come! You now have a full scholarship and a paid internship at the hospital. Do not be jealous kids. Do you remember when you mention the desire to attend a private college? Well, you are all going to that college starting next academic year." Our mother screamed, "by the way we are moving to the new house NOW and there is a moving truck outside waiting."

Imagine yourself in my shoes. How would you feel? Speechless, right?

A few years later, at the age of 43, Marthe achieved her dream. She received her diploma as a medical doctor specialized in gynecology, and shortly after, she took on to work for the World Health Organization. Not only did she achieve her goal, she was also earning a lot of money.

> *Whatever the dream, whatever the goal, there's a price you'll need to pay, and that means giving up something.*

Are you ready to pay the price for your own success? Can you fearlessly confront your challenges and turn them into a breakthrough?

# GIVE TO RECEIVE

*"Only by giving are you able to receive more than you already have."*
— Jim Rohn

"Sure, I can do it with pleasure. My credit score is high enough that it will not be any problem to buy your house in my name. Then, you won't lose it to foreclosure."

Annie Hilaire, a new member of the church, moved from Miami to New Jersey two months ago, to be close to her family. Her aunt, who pastored the church, asked Annie if she could use her credit to buy Sister Andrea's house before it went into foreclosure. Without hesitating, Annie agreed with some prerequisites. Andrea needed to make the payments on time and re-buy the property in her name once she gets a job.

I questioned Annie if she were sure about her sudden decision. She reassured me of her intention and willingness to help the church member. I was very skeptical. Although, I did not understand too much about the process but I found it uncalculated to make such a move without certainty that Sister Andrea would make the payments on time.

Three weeks later Annie finalized the contract, and Andrea was able to save her house to the delight of her kids and the church members. Andrea was a single mother in her fifties with four adult kids. She lost her job and was unable to keep up with the mortgage but thanks to Annie's arrival to the church at the appointed time, she kept her property.

Eight months later, Andrea assured Annie of her consistent and timely payment of the mortgage. Believing in her friend's integrity and honesty, she did not check with the bank. One day she received a collection call from urging her to make the mortgage payment current. At her surprise, she called the pastor and inquired about the agreement to pay the mortgage. Her credit score went from 720 to 500.

Annie called me and was wondering what to do. The mortgage payment was too far behind to catch up with her savings. Sister Andrea dissociates herself and avoids Annie's calls. At the end, she decided to take the ultimate measure by putting the house up for sale. Even though she was going through that challenging moment, Annie did not show any sign of regret to have been helpful because of her undying kindness. Unless she does not have the means, she is always ready to give. No wonder, this dear friend has always lived in abundance. No matter how tough things may get for her, she always received helping hands unexpectedly.

Giving with the openness of the heart may seem to be naivety for those who do not understand the essence of giving. Some people are professional receivers. They expect everything to come to them and appear mysteriously at the reach of their hand. There may be nothing wrong with that mindset. Giving is not just about money or material things. You can give your time, your energy, counsel, and yourself authentically and sincerely. Giving is not a transaction you do at a supermarket where you exchange money to receive an item in return. Giving is about offering yourself or anything with a sense of gratitude and service.

**You have to give freely to receive abundantly. Give without expecting a reward. Forget about what you gave, however, remember what you receive.**

Annie could not get the car she wanted because of the low credit score resulting from the foreclosure of that property. She had to hire a financial advisor who helped her improve her credit score. Today, Annie has bought her house. She lives happily and still gives to anyone in need. She is one prayerful and God-loving lady with such a beautiful heart.

How generous are you? Do you give or volunteer your time to help? Do you give liberally?

Annie always makes her vehicle available to anyone who needs it, from her coworkers to the members of the church. She volunteers her time and is a big giver. In return, I have never seen her lacking anything in her life, no matter how hard things may get, Annie is always smiling, and her motto is "Believe in God, and He will make a way where there seems to be no way." Annie's willingness to give always fascinates me. What have you given out today? How can you become successful when you are so stingy and tightfisted with your money, self, and time?

Give grace to receive grace.

# DARE TO DREAM AND DREAM BIG

*"If you can dream it, you can do it"*
*— Walt Disney*

Success is not about dreaming when you are asleep and forgetting about the images when you wake up. In this context, dreaming helps you visualize the changes you hope to accomplish. Dreaming also empowers you to bring forth those changes you saw in your dreams.

Ask yourself, "What do I want to be in this life? What are my ambitions?" Start thinking about the reasons for your birth and open your mind to the possibilities in front of you. The design of a successful life begins when you formulate your plans for a better life and have a complete faith in yourself. The ultimate achievers start with their dreams.

How big are your dreams? If you have small dreams and set small goals, you will be able to achieve only small goals. If you dream big and set larger goals for yourself, then you reach goals that are more substantial. Big dreams are always larger than your comfort zone. Which one is more important to you: staying comfortable on your brown, black, grey couch or reaching for your dreams? The choice is yours.

Dream big! Some people choose to limit their dreams to things they can accomplish confidently. They restrain their mind from projecting a higher level of accomplishment, thinking it is impossible to achieve. They limit their potentials to expand their dreams to excellence. They aim at the goals that are within their easy reach. Success calls for aiming very high and working to reach those goals. The biggest problem is aiming too low to accomplish things that are only within your comfort zones.

When are you going to find your own personal best, the best that you can be? Success is a mindset, and mastering your motivations is discovering and harnessing the powerful drive in your soul. Picture your dreams and ask which ones are the most meaningful and heartfelt; then, start from there.

Let me ask you, have you ever wondered why you are unsuccessful or why others find success more quickly? Do you feel you have not lived your hopes and dreams? Are you on the verge of giving them up? Have you caught a glimpse of a better life, but failed to go after it?

People often postpone fulfilling their dreams for various reasons:

- They do not want to achieve their dreams as much as they think they do.
- They cannot make the time to follow their dreams.
- They do not believe they can achieve their dreams
- They turn their dreams into a fantasy and live in the conditional tense.

You can't get past the limitations you create on your mind. When you believe something to be impossible, you find it much easier to quit than to carry on.

You may think you are not smart enough, or beautiful enough, or good enough. Do not let that little voice dominate your mind. What is preventing you from breaking the chains of self-sabotage and stretching to your limitless possibilities? You may want to take some time to uncover and uproot the self-destructive attitudes. You may be addicted to alcohol, TV, food, irresponsible behavior, chronic whining, past abuse and the list goes on. Now take a moment to address those issues while you start your walk towards dreaming big.

Increase awareness of your problems and be determined to deal with them in order to liberate yourself from those roadblocks. Obstacles and difficulties that get in the way of progress must be resolved to achieve a dream. We often create these issues from personal mistakes along the way that require self- examination. When you dream big, do not make excuses to stop on the way. Rather make excuses to keep on pressing. You are entirely responsible for making your dream a reality. In that process, your vision may require that you develop some skills to work and serve.

You may not be able to achieve your dreams by yourself. Healthy relationships provide an excellent support system as you follow your dreams. Friends or mentors can help one another get started on projects or vision. They can also hold one another accountable for following through. Create a dream team based on the vision, and surround yourself with highly competent people who can help you fulfill it. Select those who are already doing what you want to do.

Measure your progress toward your dream by periodically assessing the results and creating the resources to move forward. A strong relationship exists between moving toward a dream and the resources available to the dreamer.

To attain your dream, you will pass through the dash between the conception of your dream and its realization. This journey overflows with obstacles, challenges, roadblocks, and hard work. If the process itself does not bring a fulfillment to the person, then it may seem like it is not worth the trouble at all.

During the process, it is up to you whether to quit on your dreams and sit back on your couch watching TV. Achieving dreams is a cyclical process that comes from the search for learning and growth. Dreamers take time to reflect on their journeys, what they have learned and attained throughout the process. You may need to take a broad view, be introspective in choosing the next dream to follow, and develop a habit of dreaming and doing.

Many people have big dreams, yet they settle for what they already have and blame the inaction on other circumstances. They lack the tenacity to see the challenge through to completion.

What type of dreamer are you? When successful people climb the ladder, they either let things go or exchange them to reach a higher level. One dream leads to another.

You will discover the importance of your dream when you initiate and act to achieve it. People never know upfront what the complete cost of pursuing a dream will be. The price slowly unfolds as the dreamer embarks on the journey.

Success does not occur as quickly as we envision it. We keep on pressing because our dreams are too big to be abandoned in the middle of the road. They are our dreams, and we are entirely responsible for bringing them to life. Scream at the top of lungs when you feel overwhelmed by the pressure to achieve your dreams, cry as much you can when adversity is pulling you down, then rise like a champion, and ignite your inner passion and power. Awaken the invincible giant within you and move forward.

People dream for years about achieving great things or trying new activities, but they talk as if these are impossible goals to accomplish. You must move beyond merely talking about it or collecting your dreams on a to-do list. Successful people tend to be those who remain adventurous. They take risks and have no comfort zones. They make their life an adventure.

Are you the best you can be? How far can you push the limits of your achievements?

Others may applaud you for being the best in the world, but have you maximized your best? It takes courage and determination to follow a dream. That journey requires a sense of urgency to carry on the multiple tasks needed to finish well.

Go ahead. Dare to dream and dream big. Most importantly, write down your dreams so they can become goals. Make it your responsibility to achieve them. Your success depends upon that.

How often do you think about what you want and desire from life? If you fail to plan, you end up getting something different from what you yearn to experience. Activity without purpose is a drain on your life. Daily affirmations and visualization shape thought habits that can transform dreams into reality by attracting what you need to bring them into realization.

How can you take money out of the dispenser without previously making a deposit in your bank account? The choice is yours.

## IT'S ALL ABOUT YOUR ATTITUDE

*"Life is 10% what happens to you and 90% how you react to it."*
— *Charles Swindoll*

Attitude is not for sale; you do not have to spend a dime purchasing it at the store.

Attitude is a state of mind or feeling concerning a matter. Your attitude shapes your entire life. As your attitude goes, so does your life.

What does my attitude have to do with my life? You are not the first one asking such a question. Your attitude affects everything you do. David J. Schwartz said, "Attitudes are more important than intelligence."

Your reaction to any event will dictate the course of your results. Many things happen that are beyond our control. Either we call them negative or positive; our attitudes will determine whether our response will be positive or negative. It is not about us claiming to be smarter or more intelligent.

Two sisters who live in Minneapolis, Minnesota, were both working for a major corporation. However, due to the economic meltdown in 2008, they lost their job and received a severance of $15,000 each.

One sister used $5,000 to pay her regular bills for three months ahead and kept the balance in her savings. She also put herself on a strict financial plan where she spent her money only for necessities.

The other sister came home crying about losing such a job. After few days of pity party, she decided to go on a shopping spree to comfort herself. Despite their parents' advice, she spent her severance in six weeks by going on cruises and traveling. After her return, she sent out a few job applications but got no responses. Disheartened and penniless, she started going out with friends and drowned her mind in alcohol.

Meanwhile, her other sister was still sending job applications. Finally, she agreed to volunteer her time in a clothing company. Two months later, the Assistant VP got a promotion leaving his position vacant. Word had gotten around within the enterprise concerning how diligent she was with her work even though she was not a paid employee. The C.E.O of that clothing business interviewed her and appointed her as the new Assistant VP.

Indeed, your attitude dictates the course of your life. While her sister wasted her money in a short time and became an alcoholic, the first sister maintained a positive attitude and pressed forward until she had another job. Though we all have attitudes, not everyone has the same ones. You will come across many of them:

- I don't care attitude
- No attitude
- I can do attitude
- Yes attitude

Which attitude do you already have?

Which positive one do you lack, and how can you choose a better attitude?

As Brian Tracy said, "You become what you think about most of the time."

Your attitude has nothing to do with whether you are having a great day or terrible one. It affects everything around you: your career, relationship, voice, behavior and your entire life.

Nothing influences a person's day and life as much as attitude. Having a caring attitude towards people is a crucial way to energize others. Most people benefit greatly from working towards a goal with someone else and encouraging one another. Individuals should adopt an attitude of appreciation and gratitude. Those who are more grateful for their life experiences are also more likely to thrive. People who cultivate an attitude of appreciation appears to be healthier, have less anxiety and depression, sleep better, and have long-term satisfaction with life. Being successful requires choosing to believe in you. You can develop such an attitude, but not overnight. It will take time. Your attitude is a combination of your thoughts, emotions, and your perspective. It shapes how you respond to challenging circumstances. It is a determining factor in our failure or success.

Ray Charles was a legendary musician who pioneered the genre of soul music during the 1950s. Ray gradually began to lose his sight until he was blind by age seven due to glaucoma. Despite his condition, Ray chose to press on and studied music. He combined blues, gospel, and jazz to create groundbreaking hits such as *Unchain My Heart*, *Hit the Road, Jack*, and *Georgia on My Mind*. His condition could have made him into a helpless victim of life, but his attitude would not let him give up.

Individuals have the power to choose their basic attitudes in life. Then, the attitudes influence their behavior toward others. Saying, "Yes" to life allow you to open the door to more fulfilling and rewarding relationships and negotiations. Your attitude is indeed everything. What type of attitude have you chosen to embrace?

# POSITIVE MENTAL ATTITUDE

*"Success is achieved and maintained by those who try and keep on trying with a positive mental attitude."*

— *W. Clement Stone.*

Research shows that a positive mindset helps people live longer and better. It also helps them turn crises into opportunities by focusing on the present and the future, not the past. A positive attitude allows people to identify and seize new and bigger opportunities, to attract support for their initiatives and to improve their performance.

Scientists have discovered that we have 70,000 thoughts a day and about 80% of those thoughts are negative. We cannot prevent negative thoughts from invading our mind. Yet, we can select which thoughts to focus on because we have the ability to choose the thoughts we want to center on. Take your original negative thoughts and modify them by asking, "What if?"

For example, most of us grow up wanting to succeed. As a result, we are in the habit of comparing ourselves with our peers. This comparison can generate feelings of inferiority and annihilate the belief and the drive to succeed.

"Seek and you shall find." You will find whatever you are looking for in life. If you want to change your life, you have to change your thoughts process. Having a positive mental attitude is a firm choice you make to shift your mind from focusing on the negative aspects of things.

The first step to a successful life is a positive mental attitude. You cannot think or act successfully without having the mental attitude that attracts success. A positive mental attitude is not synonymous with eradicating the negative ideas. It is the process of taking the negative thought, being aware of it, and then approaching that negative information with a positive mental process.

Developing and sustaining a positive mental attitude is the key to health and happiness. When faced with a problem, view it as an opportunity and seek out possibilities and solutions.

Positive mental attitude is not synonymous with sitting on your couch and saying 'positive' things and expecting positive results. That is a pure fantasy. It is not just about thinking positive; it is rather about adopting an attitude that does not put you in a depressive, discouraged state of mind.

Positive mental attitude is about training your mind to attract what you desire.

# Chapter 5

## WHAT ARE YOU AFRAID OF?

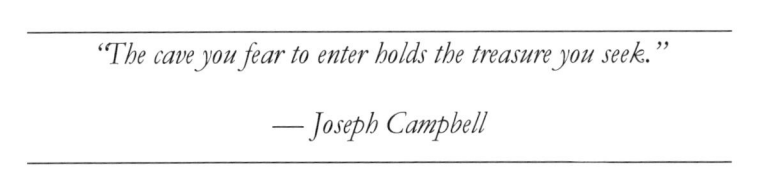

*"The cave you fear to enter holds the treasure you seek."*

— *Joseph Campbell*

Have you ever wondered how many times fear has made you back away from what you wanted?

Have you ever dreamed of moving to another city, state, or country? Have you dreamt of changing jobs? Yet you are still where you are? Are you restricted by fear?

Our fears often overcome our decision due to the mental story we make out of a fact. The story can distort our understanding and develop false assumptions about our anticipated actions. Our fears can intensify the risk of failure than the rewards of success.

Successful people see things from a different perspective. They prevent fear from blocking their action because they see it as an important part of the learning process. They feel the same fear as everyone else, yet they act anyway.

Are you afraid of rejection? How and when will you break the chains of fear? How long will you sit on your couch?

Understand that deferring an action is a failure worse than the risk of moving ahead. Do not let fear paralyze you and preclude you from learning and growing. To be successful, you must be able to deal with fear effectively.

Modern psychology teaches us that most fear is self-created and unrealistic. People often panic by imagining the worst possible scenario.

We become expert at creating fear and naming it. We have a fear of rejection, fear of failure, and fear of the unknown. There is even fear of fear. Fear is the fundamental factor that holds us from breaking through our current situation. It has caused people to back away from what they really want.

James Allen said that, "Fear kills a person quicker than a speeding bullet." Fear is a destructive weapon because it annihilates our dreams. We consent to the things we do not want and reject the things we want because of fear. We create imaginary dangers and difficulties that obstruct us from fulfilling our greatest aspirations.

We can only achieve our goals and purpose in life with healthy thoughts. Fear chokes our imagination thereby discourages us from pursuing our goals wholeheartedly.

---

*If you give fear the control of your thoughts, it invents inescapable obstacles in your mind.*

---

The dreadful thing about fear lies in its never-ending nature. No matter what you venture into doing, you will experience fear. Fear is an inevitable, yet vulnerable, part of our lives. You can conquer fear by turning it into curiosity. Then, you can explore the fear to see if it is realistic or pure imagination. Do not run away from your fear, rather use it to recognize real problems and solve them.

Will you submit to fear or conquer it with a commitment to follow your dreams? Will you remember the benefits of acting on your desire?

Can you feel that amazing emotion which comes when you achieve your objectives?

Now, compare that wonderful feeling of realizing your goals with the fear that holds you back. If your fear supersedes your goal, it is obvious you are not in control of your inner self. That goal is not big enough for you. It is less valuable to make the rewards greater than the risk; it is just a wish, not a goal, a fantasy, not a dream. Your goals should be congruent or in harmony with your heart's desires. Then your meaningful values will give you power over your fears.

When you live by your highest values, you will live an inspired life. If you want to succeed, make sure everything you do has a definite purpose with high priority. That is the fuel of courage. It propels you to become more resilient when confronted with challenges and you will also be less subject to fear.

Do you live according to your highest values? Do you even know what they are? People who very resort to motivation are those who have not yet found their highest value and purpose in life. They subject quickly to fear, procrastination, and laziness.

We get what we deserve in life instead of what we need or want. Deserving is a merit, not a gift. It is important to do things that are meaningful to you. Train yourself to do what you say, develop an unconditional and responsible integrity and live in a way that is in consonance with your highest values and priorities. Do not give up on your vision.

There are different types of fears, and you cannot just control one and overlook the others. As you progress and encounter some fear, choose not to panic. Identify and acknowledge what causes your fear, then ask yourself whether you are willing to control your mind and make the move toward that fear.

Approach your fear with a readiness to learn and take advantage of the opportunity. That will dissolve the fear and put your mind in control. Fear of responsibility is one of the best opportunities to change the course of your life. We are often afraid to take ownership and feel like hiding behind our clothes in the closet.

---

*"Everything you want is on the other side of fear."*

— Jack Canfield

---

Few weeks ago, I came across an old friend Yvonne at the Mall of America. We decided to walk to a coffee shop on the second floor. Her phone rang twice and every time she looked at it, she frowned. Jokingly I asked her if she wanted me to tell the person to quit calling her. She laughed and said they would call back in two hours between 1 and 3 pm.

"What precision!" I said, smiling.

"No, I am serious." she replied, "I am afraid to answer their call."

"Do you mean it is a bill collector calling you? Listen my dear; grant me a favor to counsel you. Will you?

"Sure," she said

"Well, are you afraid of answering the call because you don't have the money to pay, or is it something else? You are choosing not to cut back on your shopping pleasure. Are you trying to avoid the consequences of paying what you owe?" She covered her face with her hands and laughed aloud.

"I don't want to hear that now," she responded.

"I would like to suggest that you reprogram your mind not to avoid them. Instead, answer their call in a pleasant voice and explain your situation in an honest way. Make an arrangement with them and abide by it to show your integrity."

"How much money do you have in your purse now?" I asked her.

"I have $65, but that is the money I want to use to buy the pair of shoes to wear tonight to Club Seven. Okay! Whatever, Mr. Know-It-All, I do not like you anymore! Let me call them and don't you make fun of me," Yvonne giggled.

"Hello, I have seen your missed call. I apologize for not returning the calls. Anyway, I know my balance is $225...." She suddenly paused and was all ears to the other party on the line.

"Really, oh my God, you are a life saver! You mean, you are running a settlement promotion and I can just pay $90.00 to settle. Wow, that sounds interesting!" she pulled out her card and provided the information. She turned around very excited and even regretted to have avoided their calls for months.

Fear will prevent you from succeeding; it will take control of your mind and your life. You cannot allow any type of fear to take the power from you. A proper handling of fear will actually allow you to welcome fear as a motivator. It can become a driving force to trigger a bold move toward reclaiming power over any situation.

You may have come across many opportunities to increase your income but the fear of doing the actual work keeps you from accepting to get on board. Many people complain about lack of money but they are very reluctant to take actions to increase their income for fear of failing.

Are you one of them? The choice is yours.

---

*"Fear will always be a tenant in your mind, but do not make fear the landlord of your mind." – Wisdom Primus*

---

The only way to overcome your fears is to "do the thing you fear," as Emerson wrote, "and the death of fear is certain." Everyone is frightened about something anyway.

If your dreams are so simple and easy to attain, why don't you walk straight to them and take them? Did you get your degrees at school just by thinking about them or did you take the time to study various subjects, pressing your way, cutting the TV and friends' time to focus on the degrees? Though you have studied, your heart still beats when the exam day comes. Do you fake it and pretend to be sick thus, flunk the exam, or you brace yourself and go for it?

It is time to stop turning your back to fear and obstacles. Wherever you go, whatever you do, obstacles will be waiting. Do not stand still; make a move because your success depends upon the actions you take. Lisa Nichols said "Fear is not meant to stop you. It's meant to wake you up, to keep you up at night preparing and prepping for your goals"

Fear is simply a self-imposed prison that crushes the freedom of your mind, thus preventing you from exploring the fullness of your nature.

## IT IS NOT TOO LATE

*"The time for action is now. It's never too late"*

*— Antoine de Saint-Exupery*

Kofi Yiadom, a former teacher from Ghana, graduated from university in 2009. He had studied there for three years, and the interesting thing is that Kofi Yiadom was 99 years old. He said education has no end, "As far as your brain can work alright, your eyes can see alright, and your ears can hear alright, you go to school you can learn."

He enrolled at the university when he was 96 years old. Do not tell me it is too late to undertake your high priority tasks. Wanting something is different from wanting something enough to act in the face of obstacles. Kofi could blame it on his age, pretending that his brain cannot take any more information. He could blame it on an imminent death and decide to enjoy his last days on earth. Yet he defied the odds and went back to university. I am not asking you to go back to school and earn a degree; but if it is what you need to achieve your goals, do it. All I am asking is to go beyond your confines. If you really want to have what you desire, you need to get off your couch and take action now.

**It is not too late to be successful and achieve the things you have been putting aside.**

It is never late to look at yourself in the mirror: no matter the number wrinkles you have, know that your spirit is alive. You can give up easily while maintaining rigidity on your couch, but you must not allow that to happen. A boxer does not get in the ring, throw some punches, and easily win.

A perfect example is the movie "*Rocky*." Rocky Balboa was knocked down several times, and he got up only to receive more punches. However, he was able to dig deep and find the energy and strength to make a comeback and defeat his opponent.

Life will throw punches at you; it will test your resilience to pain, hurt, fear, and panic. Unless you shake off your pity parties, fake tears and irresponsible behaviors, you will remain where you are, which is whining for the rest of your life. Then, when you are in the last turn, you will say, "If I had known."

Now that your blood is still flowing, lungs are still pumping air, and brain is still operational, you need to know that you have the power to beat that cancer. You have the power to lose those pounds by starting a new diet and working out today. Yes, today! Yes, right now. You have the power to create new possibilities and a new future that will bear your personal seal.

It is not too late if you decide to acknowledge, face, embrace, and work through your fears. In your hands, lies the gift of life that was endowed to you by the universe. It belongs to you, thus use it to fulfill the destiny you will design. No one, from anywhere will hand you that destiny.

It is late at night in Minneapolis, and we are in winter season. You have just missed that last bus in traffic to carry you home. What will you do? Will you tie your shoes tighter and start walking until you see someone to give you a ride? Will you start calling your friends to rescue you or sit still and freeze to death? It is never too late to dream, to write your goals down, and to hop on the wagon to achieving your dreams.

It has never been too late. As Georges Eliot said so well "It is never too late to be what you might have been." The choice is yours.

## WHAT MOTIVATES YOU?

Do not wait for anyone to motivate you when you know your life is not where it should be.

Your motivation does not bring you what you want or desire. It is a feeling you can use to help you move forward in a direction of your choice. Motivation originates with many forces, either external or internal. Will you settle in your current place in life? Have you ever wondered if there are better things out there?

Do you need anyone to motivate you to increase your income when your bills snatch 90% of your paycheck?

Do you need anyone to motivate you when your bank account has a negative balance? You even owe the bank non-sufficient funds fees.

Do you need anyone to motivate you to lose few pounds when you feel so uncomfortable in your clothes and have difficulty breathing?

Do you need anyone to motivate you when you ruin your own mind with so many negative thoughts?

Do you need anyone to motivate you when you choose to sit on your couch whining about your past?

Do you need anyone to motivate you when you are too lazy to step out of your comfort zone and leave that pity party?

The universe is at your service to give you anything you deserve.

Stop grumbling while you have the drive to motivate yourself to make the needed changes in your life. Stop the self-pity talk because it will attract that same kind of people and situations to you. You cannot keep good friends if you whine all the time. Do something! Goodness! What do you expect? How far can you go if you hang around the same friends who are unable to lift you up and support you? Leave the whiners Club, and join the Winners Club.

Find the motivation force to propel you to act on your goals. Then, surround yourself with like-minded and better people. As soon as you know what you have to do, make use of that motivation to find the energy to reach your goals. Gear your downtime in a very effective way. How you use your downtime determines where you are going in life.

Karl, a brilliant student with the dream of becoming an electrical engineer woke up one morning and could not see. By the time they rushed him to the hospital, it was too late to save his sight. Overnight Karl became blind at the age of 23.

Surprisingly, he did not invite his friends over for a pity party; instead, he made a sudden switch in his dream. He learned how to read Braille, and he decided to embrace the direct sales business. At the beginning, his parents advised him to find another vocation. How can you connect with people you cannot see and develop a business that requires contacting people? Karl took the challenge and persisted in joining the direct sales business. After 3 years, he became one of the top performers in the company.

When asked what difficulties he has encountered, he paused and said "None." In his place, I would be mentioning thousands of challenges. He said he did not allow any negative thoughts to overshadow his determination to be the best at everything he wanted to do. How motivated are you when you sit on the couch flipping through TV channels and your dreams?

Any time you feel you are hitting a low point in your goals, take a deep breath and call for action. Pick a book or listen to an audio. Believe in yourself, and build your personality and the driving force to succeed.

Dream for yourself, create your own agenda, and fill it with new possibilities. You have to say to yourself as Og Mandino mentioned, "I will persist until I succeed in it."

# DOES YOUR SUCCESS DEPEND UPON CHANGE?

*"Adapt to change. The quicker you let go of old cheese, the sooner you enjoy new cheese"* — *Dr. Spencer Johnson*

# WHAT ARE YOU AFRAID OF?

Why would you expect extraordinary results without extraordinary actions? It is quite amazing to notice how some people act a certain way, yet they expect the greatest results to happen while their actions amount to nothing. It is about a paradigm shift from the habits that are keeping you in bondage to new habits that will propel you in different directions.

If success were free of charge, I do not envision seeing anyone struggling to attain it. It would be within the reach of any hand but it will not be as meaningful. As Ann Landers said, "Expect trouble as an inevitable part of life and when it comes, hold your head high, look it squarely in the eye and say 'I will be bigger than you. You cannot defeat me.'" It is worth taking the risks instead of being content on your couch and being lulled into a false sense of security and safety.

Do you really think that all the successful people you have heard about had success handed to them? Do you think they heard their doorbell ring and opened the door to find Miss Success introducing herself? Maybe she would say, "Hello there, Mother Success sent me to be at your service forever. We have seen you dreaming about us so here I am." Is that how success arrives?

It will not always be a smooth ride to achieve your vision, dreams, and goals. Mirage challenges will appear along the path. Pain, hurt, treason, or false promises will be waiting to hinder you. The worst thing that can happen may be unpleasant experiences; but as long as those pains and challenges are not fatal, you still have a chance at your dreams. You can still reach the top if you have the attitude to keep going no matter how hard it may get. "The only place where success comes before work is in the dictionary" said Vince Lombardi.

There is always a price to pay to attain our goals. For you, it may be going beyond your usual stretch, or feeling the burn from working out. Work on your self-improvement by reading books to educate yourself about subjects you want to master.

Imagine waking up one morning to find yourself on an island. And there were all kinds of food, except meat, whereas you are a meat lover. You cannot start your day without bacon. However, here you only have one meal choice for the rest of your stay on that island: fruits and vegetables. Are you hungry enough to eat what is available to you? Will you go on a hunger strike because there is no meat on the island? How long will you be on that hunger strike? Will you wake up one day and adapt yourself to your new diet?

Of course, you will. Your survival depends upon it. If it is paramount to achieve your goals, you must re-prioritize your habits in the direction that supports your visions, dreams and goals.

No matter how fond you are of meat, slowly you will start picking and eating vegetables. After few weeks, you will enjoy them. You will not only adapt to your new meal, but also to your new environment. You begin to enjoy your vegetable meals until you forget how chicken and beef taste.

Many companies go out of business because they were not able to quickly adapt to the new market trends. At first, we used the square floppy discs, then hard drives, and now the cloud to store information. The surviving companies are those who were able to anticipate and adapt to change quickly and repeatedly as changes came. In his book *Who Moved My Cheese*, Dr. Spencer Johnson used the metaphor of cheese for what you want to have in life. It could be a good job, a loving relationship, money, health, or peace of mind. When circumstances take it away, different people deal with change in various ways. Four characters in this delightful parable represent parts of us when confronted with change. You discover how you can let change work to your advantage and let it lead you to success.

Many animals have changed their diets, adapted their bodies to new temperatures or new climates because their survival depended upon it. As a human being, you can do the same and even more and even better. You can get off your couch, snap out of your pity party, and brace yourself to face any adversity. You can use your power to adapt and change some habits that were holding you down. It is essential to choose different habits if the previous ones are not producing the expected results.

Let others give their life away, but not you. You deserve to be successful. Failure is not a viable option. It is in fact, nonexistent because what you may regard as failure can be a success for someone.

Are you ready to change and adapt?

The choice is yours.

# Chapter 6

## FORGIVE AND LET GO

*"How people treat you is their karma. How you react is yours."* —
Wayne Dyer

Easier said, than done, right?

Forgiveness is refusing to linger on a painful event and refusing to allow it to inhibit future actions. How many times have you forgiven someone but you still hold that anger? At times, you feel like making the person "pay" for the "wrong" they may have done to you. Forgiveness is one of the most powerful actions people can take–although it does not change the past, but it enlarges the future. Forgiveness is a choice that frees us from the cycle of resentment and regret. It does not alter the past neither does it make things right nor condone what anyone has done. It shifts the present and allows us to move forward.

According to *Webster's Dictionary*, to forgive means "to cease to feel resentment against (an offender); to stop feeling anger toward (someone who has done something wrong): to stop blaming (someone)." Do we forgive or we act as if we have forgiven somebody? Feeling in this instance is not tangible. You cannot lay hands on that feeling as it is a state of mind. Thus, it is important to assess a situation correctly before letting your mind dwell on the "hurt or pain" inflicted by someone else on you.

When you forgive, to the essence of the terms, there will no longer be any blame or resentment towards that person. It may happen that you will experience a challenge forgetting the situation. You may not be able to rid your mind of the pain and frustration immediately, mainly when the issue has to do with a loved one. Forgiving people does not mean condoning or forgetting what they did to us. It means accepting what happened and freeing oneself from its weight... As important as it is to forgive others, perhaps the most important person to forgive is oneself.

Most of the time, our mind takes us back to revisit an old issue, insult, pain and those memories create a renewal of the feeling we had when they occurred. People easily let their mind drift back into those experiences thereby exposing them to emotional pain. Some are even ready to react again even though the situation happened long ago. Do not let your mind play that trick on you.

Forgiveness is not really about the person whom we claim has done wrong to us. It is about finding the courage to step out of the way and release yourself from the pain.

Are you strong enough to take the stand and forgive? Mahatma Gandhi said, "The weak can never forgive. Forgiveness is the attribute of the strong." If you do not forgive, you will always focus on the pain, anger and hurt and slowly you will sink into the abyss of revenge. Let us substitute grudges for real forgiveness. Forgiveness removes the wrinkles from your heart and gives way to healthy and stress-free living. It relieves the pressure of anger and frustration. Forgiveness frees your energy to expand. Drinking poison will not cause someone else to die, but only the one who drinks the poison. Why will you then hold grudges against someone and always be on the watch for an opportunity to make the person pay? What are your benefits? Let it go and be happy.

Rico is a man I used to trust with all my might. He was like the brother I have always wanted to have in my life. I have not hesitated to support him in his numerous breakdowns and look out for him. However, I could never fathom that he had such an envy and mean spirit towards me. But, he did...

He always denied it and lied when I confronted him. I still found it in my heart to forgive him and move on to a better connection and friendship. Many people warned me about his manipulative and cunning personality, but for the sake of friendship, I did not believe them. Gradually, I started noticing how Rico created awful situations with my other friends, blamed me and came back to laugh, chat and eat with me as nothing occurred.

Awareness of his behavior started clouding in my mind. Sometimes I caught myself in the mood of taking revenge and making him 'pay.' Then, I noticed that such attitude drains my energy rather than energizing my personality. It is the straw that broke the camel's back. Finally, I caught him having a conversation about me with a friend. I felt so devastated and annoyed. Suddenly, I realized that we did not share the same meaning about friendship. I, then remembered a quote by Wayne Dyer, "When you judge another, you do not define them, you define yourself." I decided to forgive once more and found an inner peace when I chose to detach myself completely from him.

At that time, I was reading *Living the Wisdom of the Tao: The Complete Tao Te Ching and Affirmations* by Wayne Dyer. I felt a sense of peace and relief.

---

*"True forgiveness is when you can say 'Thank you for that experience.'"* — *Oprah Winfrey*

---

Forgiving is a powerful act which liberates you from the burden or resentment, and it frees your energy. When I pulled away from Rico and let go of the anger, hurt and pain, I discovered a feeling of lightness, freedom, and joy. You are not compelled to hold on to a person or situation that causes pain. It increases the stress, particularly when the person is not contributing to your growth. My mentor Dr. Jermaine M. Davis, author of *Be Diversity Competent!*

always said "your inner circle must consist of Adders and Multipliers. You should stay away from dividers and subtracters."

Have you ever swum with someone who regularly pulls you down deep in the water to climb on you? Identify the source of the hurt and anger; forgive, detach yourself from it and let it go. "If you meet someone whose soul is not aligned with yours, send them love and move along," said Wayne Dyer.

Depending on the type of pain inflicted, our human biology encourages the revenge as a signal that we are not weak. It becomes reactionary to the threat and stimulates a payback. Ask yourself these questions:

What benefits do I get by taking revenge?

Is it worth nurturing such revenge?

What will give me more pleasure?

Holding grudges is like having a heavy bag pack on your back. Though you claim to have forgiven someone, you still carry the bag. The more you wear it, the heavier it feels until you choose to let the grudge go and free yourself from the burden of pain, hurt, frustration you have been carrying.

If you let resentment and anger stay with you, you give the power to the painful circumstances, not to yourself. Forgiveness puts the power back in our hands. It makes a space in for us to create a new future, and it points to the capacity you have to reach out beyond yourself.

Some emotional pain usually distracts us from focusing on our goals. Thus, not only we chose to forgive, but also to let go of certain things in our life in order to stay on target. As John Maxwell said, "You must be willing to give up to grow up." We tend to hold tightly to our habits, comfort zone, ego, and fears.

Above all, take a deep breath, without resentment, forgive, and let it go.

# CLEAR YOUR MIND SLATE

Ask yourself these simple questions:

- What are my beliefs or values?
- What are the people or events that shake me?
- Am I producing the results I want?
- Make a list of things that you want to let go
- Make a list of people you want out of your life.

Inwardly what am I hiding from others? Is it because you may be afraid of how people will look at you? So what? It is your life, not theirs. It is your reality for now. If you really decide to change your life for the better, this is the time to choose who and what will stay in or be let go from your life. Clarity is what we need to prepare for a better life. If you are filling up the space of your success with unnecessary, unproductive and unhealthy people and things such as pain, anger, hurt, ego, fear, conformity, setbacks, and laziness, then how do you expect to achieve your goals? How will that be possible?

Today, you may be suffering from the effect of the tough choices you made in the past. However, any serious life change requires some substantial choices. You have been used to doing things in a certain way and you feel quite comfortable with them. Nevertheless, if it is your decision to move your life in a more purposeful direction; thus make the choice to let go of the fear of letting go.

Think about how you will feel by putting away the burden of your fears, anger, and frustration, lack of money, debts, and ego… You will feel liberated, light, and free. Do not give value to things that are holding you back. Clearing your mind slate starts with one bold and brave action: look in the mirror and say to yourself with total conviction: "My name is _____ and I am taking ownership of my life now." Say it, say it again, and say it again until you are tired of screaming it. Make new choices, develop new habits now.

You cannot grow if you don't get rid of what is holding you back. People do not complain when they are comfortable in their situation. Since you are uncomfortable now, you might as well step fully into the discomfort of change. See the reality right in front of you. For how long have you been complaining, and yet you did not take an action or you took actions but did not fully follow through? Be willing to let few things go out of your life and clean your slate. Do not settle for the status quo of your comfort zone. Take the chance; take the risks because your life depends upon that major decision. One-step, one decision, one action can crack your success door open. Mom, dad, uncle, and aunties will not do it for you. The time to be a baby in the car seat is completely over and no longer will you receive cereal at your table.

Trust me, it is easier said than done; nonetheless, do it. Stop blaming your parents, friends, the government, or even your cat and dog. Are you one of those people who constantly cling to their situations and come up with millions of excuses to linger in their monotony?

You are clearly conscious of your life status but you keep on pushing it further down. Progressively you are erecting a cubicle to live in; thereby, preventing yourself from seeing beyond the barriers. You dwell in the negativity you have allowed your mind to absorb. Quite often, people may acknowledge the things that are holding them back, but they do not know how to come out of their circumstances.

It is important to seek counsel from people who are more experienced and have enough knowledge to support your change without influencing your actions too much. Do not look for someone else's opinion for they are more ignorant of your reality. Would you go to a medical doctor to teach you how to become an architect? Look for counsel, not opinion. You must be dedicated to changing your approach in order to get the results you want. The choice is yours.

If your cup is full, can you add more water? Now is the time to empty your cup and decide whether you want to pour in some apple juice, grape juice or orange juice, even milk, or better a mixture of vodka, apple juice, margarita, or however you want your liquid to taste. Now let us get to work. Empty your cup, clear your mind slate and create new possibilities.

# Chapter 7

## YOUR SUCCESS STRATEGIES

## I- GETTING THE KNOWLEDGE

*"An investment in knowledge pays the best interest."*

— Benjamin Franklin

How long can you live without eating? We are so quick to feed our body from the neck downward. How about feeding your body from the neck upward? Obviously, we all have areas that need improvement because we do not know it all. Not knowing it all is the perfect excuse to find the information you need.

Your transformation starts with you, with what you allow into your mind. Jim Rhon said, "To change your situation, you have to change first." If you have the passion for achieving your goal and succeeding, no obstacle, no challenge, no fear is big enough to stop you. These barriers may slow you down, but only while you are figuring out how to win over them. Without knowledge, you become a slave of circumstances. The greatest breakthrough in your life comes when you realize you can learn whatever you need to accomplish any goal you set for yourself. This means there are no limitations to what you can be, do, or have.

Samuel Johnson said, "Knowledge is of two kinds: we know a subject ourselves, or we know where we can find information about it." For example, if your goal is to improve your finances, you need to acquire more resources in that area:

- Read books and materials about finances
- Talk to people who are either financially free or at a higher level financially than you are.

Do not rely solely on your present knowledge because if you already knew more, you would not be in your current lifestyle. You cannot improve your circumstances by continually doing the things that created the life you presently live in. Find mentors, acquire their knowledge and apply it to your own situations. How many times have you lost ten pounds in your mind? Millions of times. You even stand in front of the mirror, tuck in your belly, and pretend you have lost weight. Everything you need to know for your better future and success is at the reach of your hands. All you need to do is to go after those materials and enrich your mind and take action.

Regardless of the strategies and knowledge you have, it is important to apply that knowledge. As it is frequently said, **'knowledge is power but applied knowledge is more powerful.'** It is only a fantasy to think that you are successful just by knowing something.

## II-DEVELOPING A STRATEGY TO IMPLEMENT YOUR PRIORITIES

*"You can practice shooting eight hours a day, but if your technique is wrong, then all you become is very good at shooting the wrong way. Get the fundamentals down and the level of everything you do will rise."*

— *Michael Jordan*

Accomplishing your dreams and goals without a plan is frustrating and unlikely. Developing a strategy to achieve your goal might seem like an overwhelming process, but if you break them it small pieces, it appears less cumbersome.

What strategies have you put in place to reach your success? Do you know why, what and how to use your talents and resources to your advantage? It may appear challenging to win without a game plan. The strategy creation follows a three-stage process:

*Analyzing the context of operation.* Focus on the type of goal you want to achieve and the reason behind it. For instance, if your goal is to become a successful business owner, you will need to know the type of business and the resources available to support you. If your goal is to become a real estate agent, take classes, read books pertaining to that field, attend workshop and learn how to become an efficient real estate agent. Depending on the arena where you want to excel, your first strategy is to be acquainted with the subject. Are there some exciting opportunities that you should pursue? As you prepare to create your strategy, make sure that you are working with an understanding of coming trends in your operating environment.

*Identifying strategic options.* What are the different things you could do to create a distinct advantage and ultimately meet your objectives? These options are how you are going to reach your goals. The strategies, action plans are all steps in the process that describe how you will allocate your time and resources to address the priority issues and achieve the defined objectives.

*Evaluating and choosing the best options.* Measure your progress to ensure your plans are performing as expected. On a daily or monthly basis, ensure that your strategy aligns with your goals and refine them as you move forward.

Develop a strong desire to achieve those objectives by keeping your eyes on the prize. Once you focus on a particular goal and actively start working it, you will notice that the universe will support you. You will attract the people and materials needed to help you get to your destination.

Michael Jordan, a five time Most Valuable Player (MVP) Awards, ten All-NBA First Team designations, and other prestigious awards, is an American basketball player who did not reach this level by luck. His competitive stamina and his will to be better led him to have those titles conferred upon him. He said, "I've missed more than 9,000 shots in my career. I have lost almost 300 games. Twenty-six times, I have been trusted to take the game-winning shot but missed. I have failed over and over again in my life. And that is why I succeed."

Contrary to the common belief, failure does not mean abandonment. Failure is definitely a key part of success.

**The only people who have not failed are the people who aren't doing anything.**

Failure should not put you in a depressive state of mind but rather push you to amend and draw lessons. Failure means lesson to the one who wants to be successful.

Every day, think differently because the life you have right now is the result of your thoughts, actions, and emotions you applied in the past. Your strategy should lead to a greater work ethic, which in turn will pave the way to your success.

Do you want to be a spectator of your life or an actual player? Spectators only watch the events happening. If you are sitting on your couch, and settled comfortably in your zone, complaining about your life, you are only watching your life happening. Then, every second that passes is forever gone. Second after second, you are getting older, letting the stream pass you by, and postponing the necessary actions to propel you toward your goals.

Do you want to succeed enough to take your power back from the remote control of your TV? To take it back from the friends who complain like you and exploit your inertia instead? From the habits that turn you into a champion procrastinator? From your laziness to get up and shake it off? From avoiding your fears and hiding behind your couch?

Do you want to quit because of the adversities and difficulties? If your life is meaningful to you, do not quit, do not give up, and do not bow down to hardship. If you have the will to succeed, you will make the way and take massive actions.

## III- TAKING MASSIVE ACTIONS

*"The path to success is to take massive, determined action."*

— *Anthony Robbins*

Take your knowledge and strategies and put them into actions. Making a decision to act toward your goals is the major step to bring them into existence. Do you become a professional football player just by watching the games on TV with a box of pizza, popcorn and drink next to you? You will only become a professional remote control handler in that case.

Be the player in whatever game you want for yourself. Whatever you desire to achieve, starts with one single step: ACTION.

Isn't it amazing to watch a full movie from the beginning to the end? Have you caught yourself someday talking to the actors on your screen or trying to put yourself in their shoes, and you said, "Run faster" or "hide."

All those people in the movie are performers, entertainers who study the scripts and as soon as the producer yells "ACTION", they start applying what they have learned. A film is a sequence of chapters, different scenes, performed in several places. After all these episodes fit together, what took the producers several hours to film, only requires about one hour and thirty minutes for us to watch.

Living your future, the way you want it, depends on preparations you do today. It depends on the chapters, sections and scenes of your own life movies. You prepare to live your future with the actions you are taking now. What are the scripts of your life? What is the story of your life? What is the movie of your life?

Re-write your scripts if you don't like the way they appear now; direct the movie of your own life according to your desire. Now is the time for you to go and work with actions that will bring the results you want. Your ambition to be successful does not come only by having the knowledge and strategies; it is the accumulation of these attributes and the actions you take.

For instance, you cannot lose weight in your head, and suddenly your body is fit. You drop that weight by getting off your couch and starting to drink lots of water, eat the right meals, put your running shoes on and get on that treadmill, practice what you have learned from the gym coach or the nutritionist.

Fantasy produces nothing but more fantasy; actions produce results. **Procrastination and fear are only the outcomes of our imagination. Whatever you want to achieve requires getting things done.** Challenging situations have already happened in your life, and I can assure you that they will continue to happen. In addition, when they do occur, they will make you better and stronger provided you decide to embrace them and keep on climbing the mountain of possibilities. Several small things have occurred in peoples' experiences, but they kept pushing them away and hiding behind the door of their success. Then, one day the cataclysm erupts, a catastrophic event happens, knocking them into a hole. They blame the whole wide world. They missed the small events that kept piling up in their lives.

Remember, the universe is not here to fight against you, but instead to bring all you need to achieve your dreams. However, you must understand it and align yourself with your values and goals and visions, your blueprints and your life.

What are your standards?

Maybe you forget them. Maybe they are buried underneath the rocks of your obstacles or your couch. Today is your day to resurrect your standards, to lay them bare and take bold actions towards raising those standards. When you raise your standards and define your must, you're resolute to going after your goals till you achieve them.

Are you walking the streets of your town with your head down? If so, look at the shape you are imposing on your body when you walk depressed and idle, letting your mind being overwhelmed with boredom. Stand straight, bump your chest out, lift your chin, and bring out your true winning nature, fighting nature, and giving nature. Today is your day to go bold on whatever you have been putting off till now. Your best time in this universe is now. Make use of it. Do not remain static. Make your voice heard and your actions seen.

Will you stop because you have failed a few times?

Will you stop because someone says you cannot do it?

Will you stop because you have seen a friend fold?

Imagine if Thomas Edison and his peers had abandoned, would you and I have electric lights today. He failed over 200 times, yet he said each failed experiment got him closer to the result. Alexander Graham Bell built on the work of people like Charles Grafton Page, Innocenzo Manzetti, Charles Bourseul, Johann Philipp Reis, and Antonio Meucci. Their failed attempts to use "make-and-break" currents led to Graham's success to invent the telephone in the late 19th century.

Will you stop fighting now because you failed in the past? Will you? You hold in your hands, one of the most precious gifts the universe has offered, the gift of resilience, coming back after falling.

Re-write your scripts and show your movie to the world. As Jack canfield said "You and you alone are responsible to take actions for the life of your dreams. Nobody else can (or will) do it for you."

## IV – GETTING THE RESULTS

*"You don't get the results by focusing on results. You get the results by focusing on the actions that produce the results."*

— *Mike Hawkins.*

Results occur either way you look at it. The results emanate from actions; actions to do or not to do what you want. There is no inaction in the universe. When you decide not to act towards a situation, it does not mean that you will not obtain a result. It just means you will not get the result you would desire. If you are sitting on your couch watching a TV program you don't find interesting, but because you are too lazy to switch the channel, your decision not to act results in you continuing to watch that boring program. Your actions or inactions will always produce results. However, they may not produce the ones you intended.

If you have a goal to achieve, and you give it a sense of urgency, you act to obtain the results or to produce the motion towards the results you want. Most of the time, people complain that they do not see the results of their actions. They think the road to progress and success is just around the corner at the next traffic light.

Imagine you have to travel on a toll road to reach a different state. You have the choice to get some coins to pay the toll, or else you must take a bypass that makes the trip longer. Besides, what if that detour is blocked further down due to constructions? What will you do? Make a U-turn and come back home? What if on your way back you run out of fuel, or you experience a flat tire. Oh, I hear you. You will call the roadside assistance.

The road to success has never been a straight 5-minute drive. It may take years to reach your destination. However, if you are not taking action steps towards the destination, you will end up stranded on the road to nowhere. Patience is a virtue to build and develop. You cannot try to be successful; invest one hundred percent effort in or you don't. Success is not about trying; it is about doing whatever it takes.

Do you wait until all the traffic lights are green before you leave your home for a trip? I don't think so. On the road, there will be stop signs, red lights; the GPS may even mislead you. You may experience some setbacks, challenges, but as long as you keep moving towards your goals, you will produce the necessary results. When you are moving toward your dreams and goals, you must assess whether your actions are bringing you closer to your destination. Your inactions will also produce results, but the question is what type of result will you get?

## V - IMMERSION

Lexi, 12, got off her school bus and walked timidly to her house, turned the knob and walked straight to her room. "Hi, mom! Hi, dad!" she said as a matter of habit, glancing at her parents who were busy discussing something in the kitchen.

"How did it go today at school?" her mother asked. Without answering, Lexi proceeded to her room, locked the door, and cried. My phone rang, and it was Lexi.

"Hey, how is my pretty mermaid doing?" I asked. Surprised by the tone of her voice, I could sense she was crying. "What's going on, Mermaid? Are you okay? Are mom and dad okay?"

Lexi is my goddaughter and since the age of three, she has loved to swim. As a result, I gave her the nickname "Mermaid."

"I guess so, always in the kitchen talking. Uncle Wisdom, I doubt their love for me. They only attended one of my swimming competitions so far. I feel so left out. I know I am the best, but all I want is for mom and dad to be there and clap for me. My other friends' parents come to support them all the time," and she burst into tears.

My heart dropped; I could feel her pain and the loneliness. Even when we are sure that we have what it takes to succeed, we need that reassurance from someone we trust. We need to have them look in our eyes and say, "You are the best; you are a champion. You can do this, and I am here for you."

Surround yourself with people who can elevate and support you. Befriend people who can give you the push to take a leap, not to pull you down by asking you to hang out with them instead of using the time to read and feed your mind with the appropriate nutrition.

Hang around people who have something you need for yourself to grow. What values are you bringing to them and what are you getting from them? If those values are not supportive and constructive, you'd better step away from that association.

You need to create an environment conducive to your goals and dreams, an environment where the subject matter is more about productive and practical thinking in line with your goals.

In the book *Mentor: The Kid & the CEO* by Tom Pace & Walter Jenkins, Tony has a criminal background and no direction in life until he meets Malcolm, a businessman, who has faced many of the same challenges. Because Malcolm is willing to share his knowledge and experience with Tony, they both become successful and significant. There are setbacks for both student and teacher, but with hope and action, they overcome life-challenging difficulties and achieve significance. This uplifting story delivers profound information in five areas: Mental, Physical, Spiritual, Financial, and Relationships.

This book shows anyone how to overcome challenges. It demonstrates the importance of sharing information about life lessons with others, so they have an opportunity to dream, grow, and establish a successful life, despite all odds. Immersion is an important part of the process of reaching your goals. By creating a proper environment and having people who can bring more values to you and help you reach higher ground, you are certain to connect and grow together. As Oprah Winfrey said, "surround yourself with people who are going to lift you higher"

# Chapter 8

## IDENTIFYING YOUR HURDLES

*"When obstacles arise, you change your direction to reach your goal; you do not change your decision to get there."* — Zig Ziglar

You are not the only one facing difficulties. We all have roadblocks to overcome. Sadly, some people decide to languish because they are too comfortable with themselves, or they lack the willpower to exercise dominion over their situations.

A hurdle runner first counts the number of hurdles he must jump over in the race, then mentally prepares himself and adjusts his speed to jump over these obstacles and win the race. You may be uncomfortable to acknowledge the hindrances you have accumulated throughout the years but don't be frustrated about obstacles because they are part of your daily life. Barriers are there to help you develop your resilience muscles if you acknowledge them and decide to face them.

Identify the challenges you experience in the physical, emotional, economic, mental, and social dimensions of your life. Obstacles do not block your path; they are your path. Ask yourself:

- What is holding me back?
- Why am I not getting a promotion?
- What type of thoughts process do I have?
- Am I hateful, revengeful?
- How long do I want to stay mad at this person?
- Why am I so overwhelmed with debts?

- Why do I feel like nothing I do, brings the results I wanted?
- Am I trustworthy?
- Am I authentic and true to myself and others?

While you are asking yourself those questions, do not answer them by justifying yourself. Instead, use the exercise to identify your obstacles. You distinguish whether your obstacles are physical or perception ones. Perception obstacles are false stories or ideas you have allowed your mind to feed on until you have engrafted them into your subconscious mind.

Your obstacles came from one of two sources. Either you knowingly or unknowingly created them or you received them from someone else.

Getting rid of your obstacles and challenges is not synonymous with irresponsibility, cowardice, or lack of personality. You cannot eliminate them as quickly as tossing a trash into a garbage bag. Instead of looking at them like a plague, welcome these obstacles with a fearless, responsible, and winning attitude. Running away from your failures will lead to more declines. The breakthrough only occurs after you identify the disruptions, create new possibilities, and turn them into productive discoveries.

Letting go of your obstacles means welcoming them. I know that may sound confusing. Let me explain. In 2006, I used to volunteer at a high school in Saint Paul as a receptionist. I noticed a young lady named Lydia. She was so quiet that you might not notice her presence near you, though she wore clothes twice her size. Lydia was obese and very timid. She barely asked questions in class and always remained in her corner. For fear of hurting Lydia's feelings by any awkward remarks, I shared my observation with Tabitha, the social worker of the school.

A few weeks later, Lydia walked to the school in slinky clothes as the other students rolled their eyes at her. Some of them turned their heads away to avoid laughing in her face. One of the students could not help herself and said, "Wait a minute, girl, what do you have on? No one wants to see all that!" A long silence ensued. She didn't just say it. Lydia slowly turned around and faced the shocked eyes. "You guys may think I am fat. Yes, indeed I am fat. I refused to admit it for years but Tabitha helped me to love myself as I am. Today, I am no longer fat. I am fluffy," and she walked to her classroom.

Surprisingly, no one said a word. Three months later when school resumed, Lydia came in and looked like a model size 8. I could not believe it. For the first time, she stopped at the front desk, showing the brightest smile. She greeted me, saying, "Good morning Mr. Wisdom, is Tabitha here today?" While she was asking, the social worker walked in the lobby. Her reaction was an immediate celebration! "Oh My God, you did it, Lydia you did it. I am so proud of you," Tabitha screamed. They hugged each other and tears of joy and gratitude dripped down their cheeks. Tabitha walked Lydia to my desk and said, "Wisdom is the one who encouraged me to talk to you and see how I could help you."

Obstacles are instruments that help you develop your resiliency and perseverance. Acknowledging them will allow you to find the right solution to fix them, and as you are solving them, you are acquiring the knowledge to use in similar settings or to help a friend that is encountering same problems. You do not get strong without obstacles.

How many times do you dream about being a dynamic success? However, you do not want the struggle that goes with building such a strong and resilient character. Building your character does not imply looking for a fight. It is about discovering your values, and dharma: the essence of your life. It implies that you are conceived out of love, your duty is to express your love by forgiving people who may have hurt you. People look at the amount of debts they have contracted, the mountain of problems they face, the bills that keep piling up on the kitchen table, but the paycheck is still the same or maybe less.

How do you get past that? What do you do?

Decide how you will face them instead of avoiding them. Think about what to do to increase your income. Either taking on a part-time job, start working on building a business…

What you choose will shape the rest of your life. Some prefer to drown themselves in alcohol consumption, drug abuse, pornography, games or silence. They choose anything that will not remind them of their present situation. However, have the problems disappeared? I hope so, but obviously not. The obstacles pile up and become thicker and thicker because nothing has been done to solve them.

You can say, "You don't know what I am going through." But how long will you say that? How long will you sing that chorus? What you may not realize is that no one cares about what you are going through other than the same people, friends, who dwell in the same types of pity party, complaining all day long and doing nothing to solve it. That type of response keeps people buried beneath their pile of problems.

*"A negative attitude toward life will never bring you success."*

*— Napoleon Hill*

On the other hand, if you take full responsibility and accept the truth about yourself, the code to break your obstacles will be accessible to you. Making a rational decision will put you on the path to understanding your roadblocks and ways to overcome them.

If you want to succeed and be relieved from your obstacles, you must refuse the conformity and use your dedication and willpower to do whatever it takes to overcome. If your barrier is emotional, accept the truth about who you are and work towards a better personality. Affirm that no matter how difficult it may appear, you are bigger than your obstacles. Some obstacles are designed to support your growth.

Roddy was a homeless person I befriended, and we usually exchanged a few words whenever I passed by. One summer, as we were driving by the area where he stands, I asked my friends to stop, and we walked to him to have a conversation.

"Roddy, my man, how is your day going? I have some friends with me, and we just want to keep you company and take the chance to get to know each other. Let's have some coffee." He quickly threw away his signboard and followed us.

"So, buddy, tell us about you. What brought you to the corner, man? Is there anything we can do to help?" my friend Ghislain asked.

He stared at him and clenched his fists as if he wanted to throw one at Ghislain.

"What, what do you mean? Do you think you are better than I am? What story of mine do you want to know? Don't insult me, brother?" Roddy reacted.

"Easy Rod, he didn't mean to offend you." I said

As I stepped in to calm him down, he started crying.

"Brother, you are the only one who always stops to greet me. I have seen hundreds of cars passing. Some people throw a dollar or scream at me to get a job.

I lost my father three years ago. I am his only child, and I grew up without my mother. She passed away on my third birthday. I used to work to take care of my father who became alcoholic after my mother's death.

"He died of cancer while I was incarcerated for drunk driving. Now, I am unable to get a job because I have so many misdemeanors and felonies. My wife left me too by the way. All my former friends told me that I could not get a job with such an extensive record although I am a great salesman. I can sell water to a well, seriously. I used to make all the bonuses. I applied for a job at few places, but whenever the background checks come back, I miss the positions.

"For the past two years, I have been homeless. To be honest with you, recently I started praying because I can hear a voice telling me to commit suicide." He hesitated and then continued, "I don't want to die now." Roddy said with a serious countenance.

"Listen, Brother, I have been thinking. I know deep in myself that this is not me. It is not my nature to be on the streets. I can do better than this, but I don't know where to start. I don't know, brother."

As he was talking, I could remember the book *Three Feet from Gold* by Greg S. Reid and Sharon Lechter. I shared with him the need to have passion and perseverance and never give up on himself.

Roddy has a motto: 'Never commit suicide in front of adversity.' That awareness is essential in the walk towards your success. Suicide in this context does not necessarily mean death but rather giving up or running away.

Roddy had identified few of his obstacles, yet he did not know where to start. The best part of his story is his ability to be truthful with himself by acknowledging his drinking and criminal records.

---

*"The secret of change is to focus all your energy in. Not on fighting the old, but on building the new,"* — Socrates

---

Our conversation continued.

"Rod, I appreciate your openness to share your story and more importantly your positive attitude. What would you be willing to do passionately without getting paid for it?" I asked.

"I can paint the world. Some people have no clue about this life. They are phony, live on debts, and full of credit cards, borrowing money here and there. I see them all. Some drive the latest cars, yet they barely make a living. I see them. They waste food, throw things away, and they do not realize that we are living beings in this world; a tree, a rock and this cup are all alive. I can paint and show it to the world."

We looked at each other, surprised by Roddy's philosophy. We all went to the store, bought some painting materials and within two hours, Roddy painted a bridge in a fascinating way. It was unbelievable. That evening, he sold it for $60. Instead of spending the money, he bought more materials and painted breathtaking images. Today, Roddy Walker has a vending spot at the Mall of America where he sells his paintings. He is married and has a daughter.

Life has never been about what you know, but how you apply what you know. Be bold.

## LAZINESS

*"If you are too lazy to plow, don't expect a harvest"*

*— Proverbs 20:4*

Laziness often drives us to complacency and inaction. While most people think they are very busy, they are disorganized, easily distracted, and unable to prioritize.

These people often have a hard time achieving goals. Are you one of them?

Ask yourself whether your procrastination is simply LAZINESS. Do you feel so comfortable on the couch that you cannot get up and grab the remote control, but you have to resort to your kids or whoever is close by? Are your goals and ambitions impeded by your laziness?

How do you expect to achieve your goals and steer your life in a fulfilling direction when you are too lazy to step up and take one little action that will improve your life and the life of your offspring?

*1. Be precise.* Articulate both the goals and potential obstacles clearly.

*2. Seize the moment, and act on your goals.*

*3. Know exactly how far you have left to go.* Use feedback to stay motivated. Shorter-term goals require assessment that is more frequent and monitoring than longer-term objectives.

*4. Be optimistic.* Believe success is possible, but recognize that success requires effort, planning, and dealing with obstacles.

*5. Focus on getting better rather than being good enough.* Use get-better goals to develop new abilities, hone new skills, and increase your motivation.

*6. Commit to long-term goals,* and do not get intimidated when difficulties arise.

*7. Build your resolution muscle.* Regularly engage in tasks you have been avoiding in order to build your self-control. Remember to replenish your willpower reserves when they are depleting.

*8. Don't tempt fate.* Consider implementing if-then plans to shield against temptations and avoid pursuing too many goals simultaneously.

*9. Focus on what you will do, not what you will not do.*

As said Sharon L. Lechter & Greg S. Reid in *Three Feet from Gold*, "There is gold within three feet from where you stand now, so stay away from self-pity, stop playing victim, and whatever you do – keep digging. It's your turn!"

*10. Quit being lazy.* Are you lazy? Look in the mirror and answer yourself. We have all experienced the good feeling of vegging out doing nothing. However, do you know this can easily lead to laziness?

We can see laziness as a general physical inactivity. It is being aware of what you must do but not developing or using your abilities to get the task done. Potential causes of laziness are due to feeling shameful, lacking self-confidence or having a fear of failure, the unknown or criticism, being discouraged. It can also result from psychological paralysis.

You can get the information you want in millions of ways unless you are willing to stagnate in your present condition. How can you yearn for success while embracing laziness?

You possess an incredible power of resurgence from stressful situations you face. You can pursue the required actions to accomplish what you want. Many opportunities await you, but you must seek them. It is not always about what you say you want to achieve. Instead of talking, take that single step toward your goal. That step, when completed, will allow you to see further down the pathway. Do you expect milk to show up on your cereal like in fairy tales? Nothing falls from the sky without cause. If it falls from the sky at all, it is because someone first put it up there! Cause leads to effect; it is the law of nature.

Of course, obstacles will occur; failures will come, challenges will ensnare you, and speed bump and stop signs will slow you down. Do you sit in the middle of the road to success just because of a few obstacles? The choice is yours.

Do not allow habitual procrastination to become another obstacle.

# PROCRASTINATION

*"Procrastination is a nasty evil spirit that lurks around the planet and it's responsible for stealing people's dreams, goals and aspirations."* — Dr. Jermaine M. Davis

"Come on, let's go. It is getting cold. We need to fly south," Mother goose shouted to her babies. Off they went, increasing altitude in the sky. The long flight south has begun. Her older son wanted to stay a bit to enjoy his meal of worms. Therefore, he did.

He forgot about the warning weather and said repeatedly, "No big deal, I still have time, I can hear other birds. I am not the only one out here. I need to finish the meal first and then fly south."

A few days later, he could not notice any more birds. "Which way is south? Where shall I go? It is too late to fly now and I cannot make it very far with this wind. I wished I had listened and followed my parents," he cried. "There is nowhere to hide. The cold winter breeze is clotting my blood."

**If you choose to defer what you can do now, you may not have the same opportunity in the future.**

Procrastinators love their comfort zone of familiarity, convenience, and least resistance. They have little discipline and are easily dreamy of different events. They lack the focus and are very uncertain, unassertive, and insecure. They like to surf in safe areas and are diffident about risk taking.

Are you a procrastinator? Easy now, I am just asking!

Procrastination is not synonymous with delay. You can postpone tasks without procrastinating by re-arranging them based on priority. When you decide to tackle the most important or the easiest ones, you only shift the order of tasks. Doing things in an order can produce greater results. That is different from procrastination.

Do not let procrastination hinder your vision. You are a courageous and forthright person, and there is a dormant champion in you. It is your duty to awaken that giant and affirm yourself. Do not surrender your dreams and goals to laziness and procrastination.

As Esaie Toingar, President Wake Up For Your Rights said "When you delay an action or pointlessly postpone activities, you are procrastinating. It is necessary to make the firm decision to see your actions through. As a result, you are spurred to accomplish more in a given time."

We give power to procrastination by yielding to our desire for ease and comfort. There is no outside cure, no pills, and no surgery for procrastination. Everything lies in you and your decision to get off your couch.

If you want to be the best and achieve your goals, you owe it to yourself to use all your strength to stand out from the crowd.

What are your excuses?

Fear robs you of your wit and ambitions. Fear blames you for the lack of money or time on your reluctance to move into success.

The lack of funds or time should be your motivators toward succeeding, not your hindrance. You can free up your time by eliminating or reducing activities that do not contribute to your values, for instance watching too much television, being glued and addicted to TV shows and playing video games all day long.

Understand the choice you have, and decide to accomplish your goals. It takes consistent actions, a firm determination, and unwavering belief to become the best that you can be.

Ask yourself these questions:

Can I allow myself to feel the procrastination?

Can I let procrastination feeling go?

When Shall I let procrastination feeling go? –Now–

Do I have authority over procrastination?

Practice this simple method and you will control that procrastination feeling and be able to take your action. By applying the choices and the promise you made, you can be the best you want to become. Once you understand the causes of procrastination, it becomes easier for you to develop some strategies with real action steps to overcome it.

Would you tell me to come back in two months when I ring your doorbell carrying a box full of all the things you want, such as weight loss, health, a CEO position, your own business, or lots of money? I doubt it.

If you respond by asking me to come back in two months, put the book down and rest comfortably on your brown, black or whatever color is your couch.

The possibilities are endless provided you are courageous and resolute enough to cast away procrastination and step out of your comfort zones.

* You can prevent habitual procrastination by sticking to your steely determination to accomplish your goals.

* Clearly define your daily goals, write down a list of actions, mark the two most important tasks, and begin immediately on the first one.

* Write a list of all the things that you have been putting off to determine whether these items are not attainable because of emotional or practical obstacles.

* Give your actions, thoughts, and goals a sense of urgency and be ready to put on your winning attitudes.

# IT IS NOT ME

> *A man can fail many times, but he is not a failure until he begins to blame somebody else.* — John Burroughs

So, who do you think is responsible for it?

It refers to the 'blame game,' consisted of finger pointing and excuses making. To blame means to say or believe someone or something else is responsible for an undesirable situation. In other words, blaming is holding other people or something else accountable for adverse circumstances, but not ourselves. Blaming always points the index finger away from us.

Some events in our lives are not necessarily our fault. Nonetheless, blaming others allows us to escape dealing with our shortcomings by denying that we had any part in the problems we face.

That habit of finding faults in others gives us the impression that our behavior is always flawless and justified. Consequently we fail to take responsibility for the solution. We often make excuses to blame others when something goes wrong.

Without seeking to understand the consequences of their actions, some people have become experts at blaming the couch, their parents, their manager, the teacher, the alarm clock, the traffic lights even the dog and cat. When you miss the nail and hit your fingers, do you blame the hammer or yourself for being a little careless? People have the perfect story made up to blame anyone or anything else for their situation.

"It's not my fault. You led me to do it. If you didn't cheat on me, I wouldn't go out last night and have sex with that girl."

I heard my neighbors arguing. The walls were thin and I could easily overhear their conversation. Listening to those words, I told myself, "Well, that is a great alibi! Blaming someone else for the act you committed. How convenient! I like that."

How many times have you blamed your friends, parents, wife, husband, boyfriend, girlfriend for your own actions?

This is the moment to embrace our responsibility objectively if we want to move in the direction of our success.

Our current lifestyle is the direct result of the decisions we made in the past. Most people run away from their reality and accountability and look around for someone else to carry their baggage. It may look like an easy exit but it's a fallacious one.

How satisfied have you been while blaming others for your misbehavior, attitudes, or negative thinking? In your hands, you hold the scepter of authority and the power to point the index finger towards yourself. If you are not serious about improving the course of your own life, you are welcomed to continue blaming others while they focus on achieving their own dreams.

If you are dedicated to self-improvement, refrain from defending and explaining every situation, but accept the responsibility to make the situation better. Instead of blaming your tardiness on the traffic jam or your oversleeping, just acknowledge that you are late. Face the consequences, be responsible and accept them with humility. Then, resolve to wake up and leave the house earlier than usual. If you continue making excuses for the past, you will not be able to improve the present, and consequently the future.

How are you feeling now? Can you vow to accept your reality for what it is?

Wherever you stand now is where a better tomorrow begins. You need to model a solution-focused attitude, where blame is irrelevant, and a focus on the future is all that matters. How long will you blame your parents, friends, your cousin, even your cat and dog?

> *"Accept responsibility for your life. Know that it is you who will get you where you want to go, no one else."* — Les Brown

People who frequently blame others consider themselves as victims who have no control over their feelings and emotions. However, others perceive them as always negative, nagging about situations, and unable to own up to their misbehaviors, choices, and poor attitudes.

People who blame others tend to get quickly angry and raise their voice. They are, in fact profoundly lacking the confidence to acknowledge their own shortcomings.

Are you that type of person?

However, those who want to succeed choose responsibility. Have you heard the phrase: 'If it's going to be, it's up to me?'

Focus on fixing the problem, not placing blame on others: "When you think everything is someone else's fault, you will suffer a lot. When you realize that everything springs from yourself, you will learn both peace and joy" said Dalia Lama (14th).

Do not even blame yourself because you will only belittle your abilities to solve issues. On the contrary, you want to acknowledge the issue at stake and assess the areas where you could have done better, learn your lessons, and move on to creating new possibilities.

The process of conquering blame and taking responsibility requires you to let go of any negative emotions and feelings, no matter how hard it may be. Your only real limitations are the ones you accept and emphasize in your mind. Stop blaming yourself and others.

# DEVELOP A SENSE OF URGENCY

*"It is not what you are going to do, but what you are going to do now that counts."* — Napoleon Hill

Most people are complacent with the status quo, and they do little to get out of that state of mind. Complacency makes people stay in the past. Such an attitude restricts us from taking the action that can lead to a successful life.

People who are complacent justify themselves by blaming others. They are afraid of change, clinging to whatever already exists without seeking better opportunities. They do not take initiative, and they stick to their old ways of doing things. At some point in our lives, we have all been complacent.

We can decide to step out of complacency and embrace a spirit of urgency instead. A sense of urgency creates the motivation to make something a new priority in your personal, professional life. The sense of urgency pushes you to think and do things that change the status quo. It is about understanding that you will not have all the time in the world to do something important, something of high priority, yet you start anyway.

You can keep on postponing going to the gym, reading a book, studying for an exam. That's postponing your life. Urgency produces energy. Every action taken with the sense of urgency produces a faster result.

Have you noticed how quickly the world is changing? A few years ago, TVs only had black and white images, then color TVs were developed. By 2011, most people had stopped using TV antennas. Now, not only is smart TV introduced, but also, we have switched from plasma, to LCD and LED TVs. We have moved from flat screen to curved TVs. 10 years ago, I could not envision having a TV where we would view our favorite shows on demand. Today there are so many features that I cannot even keep up with all the changes. Change is happening at such a fast speed.

The same is true with cellular phones. They used to be these big machines carried in a bag; but now transformed into smartphones, with a multitude of features. Every six months, new cellular phone devices come onto the market. With the sense of urgency, innovation has moved the world forward at a fast pace. Your sense of urgency, once developed, will propel you to think and act faster. It is an attitude which motivates you to be constantly on the move to achieve your objectives. Opportunities do not always show up at the door looking for us.

The longer you take to respond and act, the longer you will take to reach your goals. Smart and prompt moves create valuable results. However, do not confuse the real sense of urgency with the false sense of urgency.

The false sense of urgency comes from anger, anxiety, or frustration and it can lead people to be highly energetic. People with a false sense of urgency are always on the move. They appear to be very busy; they occupy their schedule with unproductive activities. They spend a lot of time on frivolous projects, and they tend to produce conflict with others. People with a false sense of urgency can easily be mistaken for those with a true sense of urgency because both appear to be busy.

Which category best describes you?

Are you complacent? Do you have the false sense of urgency with lots of activities, but little productivity?

Increasing your sense of urgency may be difficult if you procrastinate. Having a lot going, is not synonymous with getting something done or being busy. The sense of urgency is more about working to create and generate so that you do not put off until tomorrow what you can do right now.

The sense of urgency helps you move faster in the direction of your goals and not to give way to distraction. If you want to get ahead, you must get started and follow through. When you decide to change the course of your life and achieve your goals at any cost, you will feel the burning pressure to get on it right away. You create that sense of urgency.

People do not always act as they should when they have enough time. They wait until the last minute to work on their goals. Have you experienced a time in college when you waited till the eve of your exam to study?

The use of the sense of urgency takes the last minute pressure off your shoulders. You develop the enthusiasm to get what you desire right away because you only have the present in your hand. A winner does not wait till the stakes are high before starting to move toward the destination.

A winner wins before the race even starts. The universe has deposited in everyone the seeds of a champion. Being a champion is not by luck but an effort. However, we have to awake that champion in us and allow it to surface. Do not let your inner hero stay hidden until your last day. Don't be caught up with "I tried" mentality.

Do not give up on yourself. Put one more foot in front of the other, one more and one more. You have it in you to enlarge your potentials.

Will you wait for an opportunity before getting ready to take advantage of it; or you get prepared and ready before the opportunity arises?

Challenge yourself and stir up your sense of urgency, especially when your mind keeps saying, 'I don't feel like doing it.' Allow your thoughts to feel the urgency of your daily goals.

- Communicate with urgency.
- Bring out the winning attitude.
- Feed your mind through constant learning.
- Find breakthroughs in breakdowns.

How can you create a sense of urgency to handle your priorities?

- Eliminate inefficient practices
- Become a get-it-done person.

# Chapter 9

## PAST, PRESENT, AND FUTURE

## YOUR PAST

*"The failures of the past must not be an excuse for the inaction of the present and the future."* – Martin Luther King, Jr

People are married to their past, make love to their past and have children with their past. The events in your past have already occurred. The past remains in the past tense.

Samira came back from work one day and noticed that her husband Rahman did not pick their kids up from the day care. In her panic, she contacted the hospitals and the police to no avail. Three months later she received a private phone call:

"It's me, Rahman. I am no longer coming home. I can't take it anymore. I am through...."

"Really, you left us for another wo...?" Samira could not finish her sentence when the line went off. There was no number to call back. She was so devastated, playing the seven seconds conversation in her head repeatedly, trying hard to make sense out of the 'unpredictable' situation. At least she knows now that her husband was not dead; he simply decided to leave them without notice. It was the last time she heard from him.

Three years later Samira decided to move on with her life and meet another man. After four dates with four different men, she was unable to grasp the reason why none of those men has called her back for a second date. One day, I attended a seminar where I met Samira. Our conversation went from the seminar to jobs, swinging by kids and landing on relationship. We agreed to meet for coffee. As I was taking the first sip of the dark looking liquid and savoring the taste, Samira asked me if I would leave her in case we decide to be in a relationship.

"Welcome to the relationship interview." I laughed inwardly. "What do you mean Samira?" I asked.

"What I meant is very simple, either you answer or you don't. The content of your response will determine whether I shall sit here with you or go home to my kids." She said aloud, raising the eyebrows of the neighbors at the other table.

"Wow, wow, someone is on the edge. Easy lady, I don't think this is the right place for such a conversation. Let's go for a walk, shall we!" I suggested and motioned her to follow me. We went out for a walk and I asked her: "Miss, I appreciate the fact that you want to have an immediate clarity. I believe something else is the reason for such an abrupt question with that tone of voice. I respect your reality and if you don't feel comfortable to share, I'll definitely understand and let you be."

"It is hard to explain," she yelled at me. Slowly she embarked on expounding how she could not fathom the reason why her ex-husband disappeared from their life overnight and why none of the gentlemen she met, called her back. She was convinced that she will be single for the rest of her life. As I was observing her countenance, she looked so drained, exhausted, and angry. She appeared to have gone through so much and could not help crying while she was narrating her experience.

For over three years, Samira has been carrying the burden of her past, the unanswered questions about her ex-husband's abandonment. There seemed to be no space in her heart to welcome any relationship.

Mostly we respond to our life experiences based on what we are prepared to believe in. Moreover, what prepares what we believe is our experience. Would it be so easy to click on a button and undo our experiences and the pain we went through?

We only have limited hold over our experiences. However, we do have a total control over our attitudes and responses to our experiences. When we were children, we didn't choose those experiences, but as we become adult and more aware of our life, we choose for instance, who we marry – in some cases, the parents make that choice for their children-; we choose our jobs, friends. In any case, can Samira reverse her experiences but she can progressively learn how to reprogram herself and create new experiences and attitudes.

Samira has been living in the past by making stories about the reason why her ex-husband left them. She portrayed herself as a faithful wife, who takes care of their kids, the house and is good to her man. However, when it comes to describing her husband, he was mean, stingy, did not laugh much, and screamed at her and the kids, unfaithful and irresponsible. The list went on. That defense mechanism she developed, helped her to become so stiff that her first question after meeting someone is "will you run away from me someday?"

Samira is simply living in the past, constantly referring to her past experiences and events. I commiserated with her as I felt her frustration. I was very concerned about the limitations that veiled her mind.

"I am pretty sure you will also leave me, just like my ex-husband and the other men I went on a date with. My life is miserable, monotonous." She affirmed.

"It's been three years since your ex-husband left. Have you stopped breathing, eating, and taking care of your kids?" I asked her.

"What a silly question you are asking?" She replied with a smile.

"I know it's a silly one," I continued "Well, if you allow me. As long as the world clock hasn't stopped after he left, why do you stop your own clock? There is neither good life nor is there a bad life: life is just life. Either you have the ability to control some events or not, your attitudes are the ones that will determine how far you will go with or without the events. It does not matter the strength or energy you have, but rather the attitudes you have chosen to develop. Close your eyes; breathe in and breathe out; tell me how do you want your life to be from now on? Where do you want to be and how do you want to see yourself Samira?"

With tears dripping on her cheeks, she responded, "I see myself free from the burden, happy and full of energy; I see myself laughing and smiling every day with my kids. I know he is not coming back and I want to let it go and be happy"

*"The past is a place of reference not a place of residence."*

*– Willie Jolley*

I held her hands and asserted, "Choose to create the possibilities of the type of life you desire; choose to substitute the pain with joy; choose freedom and a limitless life. It is not about what your ex-husband did; it is about you, choosing not to settle your life based on your experiences but to create a new future and new experiences. Now open your eyes and be grateful for your past, be more grateful for your present. Change and focus on yourself and become the loving person, the loving mother and future wife you desire to be and have faith in yourself and others."

How do you expect to live your life today while you are holding on to the past like a bull dragging a plow? How far can you go in your life when you sit on your couch buried in thoughts about your past events, pain, hurt, anger, frustration… you name it yourself. Many people worry about what has already happened and cannot be changed; they worry about the future and fear what has not yet happened.

Obviously, we have all been through situations that have deeply affected us, made us feel depressed and rejected. However, you cannot live in the past forever. By releasing the hold off your past and learning to trust the future, individuals are free to turn their attention to the present moment, the place of power.

It takes strength to forgive the past, courage to trust the future, and discipline to stay in the present. The rewards can be great: inner contentment, mutually satisfying consonance, and healthy relationships. Don't be one of the people who make up stories to justify what had happened in their past and consequently their present behaviors are deeply affected. Anger, betrayal, frustration, and grudges we carry from our past limit our options, influence our relationships and affect our experience of living fully.

"The good news is that, at any time, you can stop thinking about, discussing, and rehashing the past. You can let it go and begin thinking about your goals and your unlimited future." Brian Tracy. Dwelling in the past can be self-destructive. It prevents people from enjoying the present and planning their future.

---

*"You can't change the past. You can change the future. Would you rather be influenced by something you can't change, or by something you can?" — Jeff Olson*

---

In *The Slight Edge*, Jeff Olson observed that most people live with one foot in the past, saying, "Only if things had been different, I would be successful." They keep the other foot in the future, saying,

"When this or that happens I will be happy." Thereby, they completely ignore the present, which is all we really have.

Dwelling in the past does not change anything. In fact, it interferes with people's ability to become their best. You actually live your past in the present. It is far better for people to focus on the present and think about how circumstances in their personal and professional lives can change for the better.

## YOUR PRESENT

---

*"The future never takes care of itself; it is taken care of, shaped, molded, and colored by the present. Our todays are what our yesterday's made them; our tomorrows must inevitably be the product of our todays."*—Dennis Kimbro

---

The present moment is the only moment we ever have, while the "Now" is the only living state we possess. Living in the now is living in the moment you are reading this book. How are you living your life now? Are you gratified? Do you live your life in a satisfying way or would you rather live your life in a different way?

Make this moment an emotional success and keep your attitude as pleasant and cheerful as possible. Learn to live fully in the present because the outcome of future situations however, can be determined by the actions taken today, which you can easily control.

How do you expect to live a joyful, fulfilled life today if you did not plan for it before today? Most people live in the present and look forward to the future without understanding that the future is actually prepared in this moment. Depending on where you live, you may have all four seasons: winter-spring-summer and fall or rainy season and dry season. This has been a fact for millions of years. When you are in a tropical area and it is the dry season, you know for sure that the rainy season will follow. Your life does not operate like the seasons of the nature. You own the compass of your life seasons and you can choose the season you want to create without awaiting circumstances to impose it on you.

Your present life unbelievably is the consequences of the way you have either planned or not planned it. If you do not plan your tomorrow today, when you get in that tomorrow which is becomes your present, how will you live in it? Would you rather live a life like a leaf tossed back and forth in the wind? The choice is yours.

In the *Power of Now*, Eckhart Tolle said, "You cannot find yourself by going into the past. You can find yourself by coming into the present. Life is now. There was never a time when your life was not now, nor will there ever be."

Do not immerse your mind in the excessive thinking of the past because only the present can free you. Time is passing anyway, so decide how you will spend it and where you want to end up. Your present is where great things can happen.

As long as your attention is in the present, your purpose for the future will manifest, because the future emanates from the present. If your current life is not reflecting the image that you desire, it is not too late to create the opportunity for the future. Look at yourself in the mirror and say it aloud: 'I have had it! It is enough! I cannot keep on living this way! Today is my day!'

Why would you worry about a day other than today? Are you so certain to wake up tomorrow or even walk in two minutes? What is viable is your present, this moment you are holding the book in your hand. Live in the present and work to enjoy what is going on as it happens. Accept the present as a gift because each individual's time in this physical world is limited. It may appear challenging for you to stay focused on the present moment. Do not obsess about yesterday and do not be seduced by the promise that tomorrow will be better.

Facing the present allows you to conquer adversity and create your own defining moment.

> *"I live in the present. The future, don't know it. The past ain't got it anymore."* — Fernando Pessoa

Would you rather let your circumstances, challenges, obstacles, barriers, pain bury you in the bottomless pit? Like a bud in spring, sprout to the fullness of your abilities and conquer other grounds. You will then leave an everlasting legacy through your seeds. Do not depart with your head down. Go down knowing you have given all you have in you. Let the burning fire out to melt the snow and warm others. You owe it to yourself to live it all in the present. Consider your present life as the couch you are sitting on and as you are looking through the window, design your future the way you want it to be, because pretty soon, that future will become your new present and life goes on. The actions you decide to take in today will determine the outcome of your future.

> *"Yesterday is gone. Tomorrow has not yet come. We have only today. Let us begin."* – Mother Teresa

Look to the past for useful lessons. This does not mean dwelling on or reliving past failures or carrying the past with you. Live only in the present. This does not mean settling on or taking it for granted. Be excited about your future. This does not mean living in a fantasy or utopian dreams.

Take a clean and immaculate board and draw your future the way you want it to look like.

# YOUR FUTURE

*"The future depends on what you do today."*
—*Mahatma Gandhi*

The future belongs to those who prepare for it because the word future ultimately becomes the present. Develop the ability to visualize future goals in order to create a mindset that makes your ambitions possible. Nevertheless, people fall prey to a lifestyle that transfers their past into their future and they live as if they have their eyes in the back of their head.

I remembered in my teenage years, asking a girl out and she turned me down and told me that I was not her type. Now, you are laughing. Aren't you? I felt so crushed in my heart. I understand she may not be interested in going out with me. But what does she mean by I am not her type?

I felt so ashamed, belittled and inexistent that I secluded myself for days. For several weeks, I lived with that event in mind to the point that I could not dare asking any other girl out for a while.

What happened is a simple illustration of how people live their past in the future. Though the situation happened months back, I projected the results in my future, holding myself from asking another girl out with the assumption that she will say, "I am not her type." I was using my past experience as a yardstick for deciding the future, thereby preventing myself from breaking with the past and making a move towards another girl.

Does that ring a bell? Not that you may have experienced the same situation, but similar cases where you projected a frustrating situation from your past into your future that prevented you from taking action.

In order to be successful, people have to visualize what they want to accomplish in the future and take a bold move. If you don't plan your future by anticipation, you will end up living it by apprehension where someone else decides how it is going to be for you.

If being successful is so important to you, then you will begin each day with thoughtful planning about how to utilize your time, from both short-term and long-term perspectives. You will base your present decisions on future goals since having clear visions of the future will guide your activities in the present. You will feature in your personal values, visions, and missions when making decisions on how to spend your time.

Your parents did not give birth to you with a stamp on your forehead that reads, 'this child will amount to nothing, and he or she is doomed'. On the contrary, you were and still are a joy in their lives, no matter how things may get now, deep in their heart, they value you, and they love you, and want nothing but the best for you. When you came out of the womb, your eyes were glowing with the light of greatness and hope.

The universe has made everything available for you to use and enjoy in designing the type of life you desire. Just like the creative artist who uses his brush and different paint colors to draw on his blank board, you must design your future based on the dreams and goals you have and how you want that future to look like.

---

*"Your future is created by what you do today, not tomorrow."*

— *Robert T. Kiyosaki*

---

Imagine being in your mother's shoes when she found out that she was pregnant. Regardless of her sadness, excitement, anger depending on the circumstances, she started thinking about whom the baby will look like, and as the days go by, what type of clothes to purchase.

As soon as she found out about the sex of the baby, the excitement became bigger. She visualized the baby, began to shop for the clothes, shoes, hats, you name it. Every thought was fixated on that baby. She got into the discipline of the types of foods she might avoid or eat more. Sometimes she felt the weight; changed her position when she sat or lied down, uncomfortable feeling, sickness… She went through it all and even in her worst pain, she still held on with excitement until you were born.

If you are interested in building a successful future, just like the pregnant lady, the artist, though you may experience challenges, you need to stay on track because a planned life is worth living in. Here you are today, bearing the name of your parents with their blood running in your veins, are you ready to go through it all to give birth to your designed future?

Can you write anything on a board that is already filled with caricatures? There will be no space to put any additional information. If your future is already filled with your past experiences that you still drag along, how would you design that future at your will? Where will you find a space on the board to hold new designs? It is true that we need to learn from our past experiences in order to create a better future, but not to carry that past like a purse or a wallet. Clean your slate and create the future you want to live in.

*"Learn from your past, live fully in the present, and create your future." – Wisdom Primus*

## WHAT IS YOUR "I AM"?

"I AM" is the combination of the subject "I" and the verb "to be" in the present tense. The present tense is one practical tense that defines the moment, the present, and the 'now'.

"I AM" has connotations, not just in the conjugation of the verb to be, but more importantly in our understanding of who we are. As I mentioned earlier, the universe has given us the power of the spoken word so we can give life to language.

If you want to achieve your life dreams, be more conscious of how you use "I AM." When you describe yourself using the power of "I AM" statements against yourself, you are sending an invitation to those words to come and feast in your life. Some examples are:

"I AM unlucky,"             "I AM unsuccessful."

"I AM upset,"               "I AM unfit"

"I AM unattractive,"        "I AM fat"

What follows the 'I AM' has to be well thought, well articulated and believed. Each word has a definition, a meaning and when we use it, we act emotionally to match the meaning of that word. Thus, shouldn't we be more mindful of what we say? Shouldn't be more concerned about the contexts in which we use those words?

The words you choose to place after I AM should be carefully examined, understood and utilized appropriately in order to avoid causing harm to yourself. People frequently say, "I AM busy," when in fact they simply want to avoid doing something. Why can't they simply be honest and say, they do not feel like doing something instead of confusing themselves with "I am busy"? What type of blessing, grace, and abundance are they calling upon themselves if they pretend to be so busy?

Recognize that the personality you are calling upon yourself will always come to find you. I learned it the hard way. I used to say,

"I am busy," not because I was actually busy, but because I did not want to get off my couch. I have read some of Harvey Mackay's books such as *Swim with the Sharks without Being Eaten Alive*. I even offered a copy to a good friend of mine Calvin. One day he called me and told how great it felt to attend Harvey's seminar and all the knowledge he received during that event.

"You must be kidding me," I angrily said, "You didn't even call me."

"I am sorry Wisdom; you seem to be busy all the time. Whenever I reach out to you, your answer is, 'I am busy, I can't' so I assumed you would be too busy and would not have the time to attend. As a matter of fact, I had an extra FREE ticket," Calvin said. I felt so devastated and angry at myself. I couldn't blame my friend for not calling me. I projected a constant adjective that was not conducive to such an invitation. Calvin knew me as 'Mr. I AM busy' and simply assumed that I was busy. I had often said those words to him and now they have taken the space, and I missed that opportunity.

Be very mindful and careful of what you say because it will create the exact environment and feeling you are calling for.

When you wake up in the morning, say to yourself with conviction, "I AM grateful; I AM patient; I AM beautiful..." Then, pay close attention to how your day goes. "I AM" is said not only verbally but also with faith and enthusiasm. Who do you say you are with your "I AM" statements?

"I AM" can be said in three major cases:

1 - *I AM kind/patient...*: that is verbal affirmation

2 - *I AM kind/patient...*: close your eyes and visualize what being kind or patient means to you. You are then saying through the power of visualization that you are kind or patient. That is visual affirmation.

*3 - I AM kind/patient...*: feel it deep within your soul and spirit that you are emotionally kind or patient. Think about what it means to feel kind/patient. How does it affect your facial expressions, your shoulder positions, and your walk? That is emotional affirmation. Every day, affirm, visualize, and "emotionalize" yourself into being the person you want to be by using I AM ...... [*That which you want to be.*]

I AM, in the deeper and spiritual sense is the mystic name that God revealed to Moses in Exodus 3:14 (KJV) And God said unto Moses, I AM THAT, I AM and He said, "Thus shalt thou say unto the children of Israel, I AM hath sent me unto you." I AM in this case stands for the true nature of God. Take dominion over those words and use the power of spoken words to materialize your dreams and goals. When you wake up in the morning, whatever word you add to 'I AM', will depict the actions you are calling for and the results you will get. For instance, when you say to yourself:

"I AM tired." you will feel indeed tired. How about replacing it by saying, "I am in need of energy to finish this task."

"I AM sick." You will feel sick and sluggish all day.

"I AM poor." You are calling for more situations to confirm that you are indeed poor and impoverished. You will find yourself deprived of the power to create the riches you want in your life.

"I AM broke." You get what you ask for. The waitress will not serve you fish sandwich if you request a chicken sandwich. Your mind patterns to whatever you internalize.

"I AM ugly." No matter how much make-up you put on or how many showers you take, you will always remain as what you call yourself.

---

*"The only way things will change in your life is by changing how you see and do them."* —*Wisdom Primus*

---

So, start using the power of 'I AM' appropriately. However, what you think and feel about yourself will determine the type of life you will live. The words you speak will create your reality.

Let's practice this instead:

"I AM grateful, fearless, beautiful, and handsome."

"I AM patient, honest, appreciated."

"I AM expressive, able, and talented."

"I AM important, successful, accepted."

"I AM empowered, intelligent, and dedicated."

Your outer reflection comes from within yourself. Focus on your true nature, the nature of your "I AM," and bring out what you want in life.

There are 24 hours in a day and that reality will never change. So why some people say they have no time as their day is less than others'. The most successful people have the same time as you do. It is all about what you focus on in your "I AM". You will find whatever you are looking for and the stories you tell yourself about yourself create either the limiting beliefs or the expansion in your life. Where is your focus?

Have you had those moments where you can't find your keys whereas they are right there in front of you or you put them in your pocket? Then you have to take a minute, rethink step by step till suddenly you remembered exactly where you put your keys? Did your eyes see the keys on the table? Yes, they did, but your mind would not let you perceive it because you kept telling yourself a story over and over 'I don't know where the keys are'. At that moment, your brain creates a blind spot blocking you from easily seeing what was right in front of you. The only thing keeping you from achieving what you want in life is the story you tell yourself about why you have not accomplished it.

"I AM not ready", "I will do it tomorrow", "When I have more money", "I AM not old enough". How can you achieve anything right now if your story has always been about what "you are not", "what you can't do" "what is wrong with you"?

*"Separate yourself from the story you have created from your limitations and embrace your true capabilities, the facts. Come up with new stories and build a new life" - Wisdom Primus*

You have the abilities to become the greatest YOU. The strategy is to rid yourself from those limitations and design a new life, a life of a winner, a life of a conqueror, a life of courage, a life you enjoy.

Based on what you want to become and achieve, take some moments before you go to bed and speak it with affirmation, visualization, emotion and belief.

## THE POWER OF VISUALIZATION

*"If you want to reach a goal, you must see the reaching in your own mind before you actually arrive at your goal." — Zig Ziglar*

The act of visualization can turn positive ideas into positive realities. Visualization of future goals creates a mindset that makes an individual's ambitions possible. Understanding what you specifically want is the foundation for accomplishing goals.

*Visualize in the present tense.* Using the power of visualization is imagining yourself already having the results you desire. Two words connect you with your future. Notice *'yourself'* and *'already.'* You see your future as already present.

In the process of visualizing your goals, it is crucial to see yourself achieving what you want. It is not enough to see your dreams and goals if you do not include yourself in that image. How would it feel to visualize abundance but see someone else having it instead? Your visualization must focus on seeing yourself in possession of that abundance. You positively and explicitly represent what you have visualized.

Visualization empowers you when you go to a car dealership and sit in the driver's seat. Seeing yourself behind that wheel is a call to the universe to guide you into the actions needed to turn that visualization into reality.

When I landed at the Minneapolis-St Paul airport and as I was walking toward the taxi, I saw this shining black Chrysler 300. I could not take my eyes off of it. I immediately pictured myself in the driver's seat with a silver watch on my right wrist; wearing a white long sleeve shirt and a pair of light blue jeans. I saw myself in some flat polo shoes. I could smell the CK 1 cologne on me. That visualization began to take effect.

For some reason, I started seeing that car everywhere I went and respectively, I saw myself as I described earlier. When you tap into the visualization power, your reticular activating system starts filtering the massive amounts of information our sensory organs are constantly throwing at us. It selects the ones that are most important for our conscious mind to pay attention to. It has a very important role: it's the gatekeeper of information that are let into the conscious mind. Thus, whatever we really focus on starts appearing more to our eyes.

Knowing that the car will not fall from the sky, I went to volunteer at a school until I found a job. I saved money and bought my first Chrysler 300, black color with leather interior. In addition, I had on exactly everything I mentioned.

As Shakti Gawain wrote in her book *Creative Visualization*, "You don't need to understand or figure out how this will happen, or try to decide the best way to work it out, rather assume it as working out for the best, and let the universal intelligence take care of the details."

The subconscious is impressed with what you see and what you feel as if it were already a reality. The function of visualization is to say through mental pictures and feeling that you possess what you set your mind onto. Use affirmation in your visualization through a strong positive statement that it is *'already'* so.

*Avoid the use of negation such as 'not' in your affirmations.* My friend Tesia McAfee always says in her prayers "She does not want a man who smokes, who does not have a decent job, who does not cheat and does not treat his lady right and does not spend money on his lady." Amazingly, all the men she comes across possess the characteristics she does 'not' desire. Instead, I invited her to use positive affirmations of what she wants and desires. Today she is one happy lady building and living her dreams on strong and positive affirmations.

*Make sure your affirmations are in congruence with your values.* Feel it deep inside of your heart and speak it out.

Everything in our physical universe is made of vibrations of energy including our thoughts. Therefore, any idea repeated in our conscious mind makes an imprint in our subconscious mind. Once in it, our thoughts vibrate, emit energy and attract the people, the circumstances and the synchronicity of what matches the image within. Use your mind power techniques such as visualization affirmations and you will begin to take ownership of your life.

*Practice visualization with music and tranquility.* Choose a lulling instrumental music, and with eyes closed, let yourself go into deep relaxation. Visualize yourself in the midst of your dreams, your goals, and your success. Then, progressively inhale them, embrace them, and feel them. Repeat this process every day.

*Take five to ten minutes a day and imprint empowering beliefs into your consciousness.* Practice and repeat what you want until it deeply engrafts into your consciousness. For instance, "I have unlimited power at my disposal in the universe, "I am a peaceful person," or "I build a successful business." Whatever your affirmations are, repeat them daily and progressively until they become as much a part of your mind as your multiplication table. Nevill Drury, in his book *Creative Visualization to attain your goals and improve your well-being*, said, "Our inner world of personal belief is shaped by years of specific experiences and responses, which has gradually built up a picture of who we are, and what we can achieve."

Go over your list of affirmations and feel yourself being successful. Visualize it as if it is happening now.

*Remove any doubts, resistance, negative self-talk hindering your thoughts from creating your visualization.* For instance, you see a beautiful house up the hill, and you feel and believe that it is your house. As you are about to create that affirmation, a little voice in you says, "You must be dreaming! You only make $9.75/hour! You have so many debts, even working 24 hours a day, you would not be able to pay off that house. Besides, here you are thinking of owning this house. Go and own it. You'd better think about what you will eat for dinner. As a matter of fact, I am hungry now." Take a hold over the little voice in you and make your affirmations vivid and bold.

Be focused on what you want to accomplish and be persistent and passionate. Visualize with a smile on your face, and create the feeling of happiness when you are saying your affirmations.

*Be relentless. Recognize the fact that you will face adversity.* When you want something, do not expect people to be on board with you immediately. Keep your mind on the goal you want to reach and the challenges will fade away as you progress towards your objectives.

An excellent way to achieve your goal is to fill your subconscious mind with visions, images and thoughts of your ideal life. When you visualize yourself in a certain scenario, the brain functions as if you were really in that scenario. It helps you prepare for it and grow accustomed to the scenario. Visualize yourself at your ideal level of success. What kind of house will you have? How will you feel? How will you act? When you visualize success, you begin to see the opportunities that lie around you to navigate you to the path of what you want out of life.

With regular visualization, the subconscious mind finds solutions to problems and is constantly looking for useful information and connections you might need. Creating a picture board of inspiring people and images of goals is very helpful. Take the time each night before you go to bed and visualize yourself acting the way you'd like in situations you've had difficulty with in the past, or might have difficulty with the next day. Before retiring at night, take a minute and ask yourself "what extraordinary thing have I done today? Have I completed my goals today?

# THE LAW OF ATTRACTION

*"I attract to my life whatever I give my attention, energy and focus to, whether positive or negative."* – Michael Losier

"I am not feeling well, I can't make it to work today," Lindsey coughed as she was informing her manager over the phone that she could not report to work.

"It is okay, go to the hospital or take some medicine and get some rest; I will have another colleague cover your shift. Anyhow, it does not seem too busy today. Take care of yourself," the manager responded.

She put her phone down and made sure the call ended. It was Friday. They all burst out laughing. Lindsey's best friend Debra shouted, "Girl, you nailed it! You should be an actress. Let's go party!"

Few hours later, Lindsey started feeling a bit nauseous and feverish.

Is that karma? Call it what you know or want.

Have you ever experienced such a feeling? After bluntly lying about your health, did you start feeling the same symptoms you described? Have you experienced a time you used your kids or family member's sickness as an excuse; then they started feeling sick afterward?

You called for it to happen. Karma or not, it is the result of the vibrations you attracted to yourself. It started with putting yourself into the thoughts and feelings of a sick person, mimicking how you talk when you are sick. To make your story seem more valid and convincing, you force yourself into the attitudes and actions that make it more believable. The law of attraction operates that way.

"Ask and you will receive."

Our mind is shaped by our thoughts, so our thoughts become the law of our life. Our thoughts are energy, and energy is everything. Repeated thoughts in the conscious mind make an imprint in the subconscious mind. That attracts the people, circumstances, and events to match the images inside you.

The law of attraction operates in a very simple way. If you do not plant flowers in the garden of your mind, you will forever pull out weeds. Once you concentrate on what most inspires you, only then can you focus and work towards it. You will see the opportunities you might have overlooked; you will act on the possibilities you might have neglected until you fulfill those goals. We attract into our lives those things that are the core of our attention.

Beware of what you allow in your mind. We live in a world where all types of plants grow, and dependent upon the plants that you want, you uproot those you do not want and constantly guard the ones you prefer from being invaded or contaminated by other undesired plants. That's your task to carry everyday of your life.

Control your conversation. Do you have those friends who always come to you and complain incessantly about money, debts, poverty? The more that conversation continues, the more of the same attraction will come to them and consequently, it will affect you.

The more you complain about debts and lack of money, the more of that situation will arise. Instead of focusing on debts, how about you converge on increasing your income, finding other legitimate ways to bring more resources that can allow you to make more money? With more income, you will be able to pay off your debts. Take 15 minutes a day and practice taking dominion over your thoughts and reprogramming them to focus on what you want and desire in life by asking yourself few questions:

What do I want today?
What would I like to manifest in my life today?

How do I want my day to be?

# Chapter 10

## MAKE CHOICES

A leaf in the wind is blown away in any direction. Do not let your life be an aimless generality. Success does not occur by mere luck or magic. It requires some choices to create the proper environment to welcome it. Thus, the choices you make can either bring you closer to your success or take you further away.

## CHOOSE YOURSELF: LEARN AND GROW

The self-choice consists in making yourself the priority in your decision to achieve whatever you define as your success. On the airplane, when the flight attendant goes through the safety manual, you hear her or him say, "Put your oxygen mask on first before helping others in case of emergency." Similarly, how can you save someone from drowning when you don't know how to swim?

It is important to focus on yourself and your decision to reach the new destination you are creating. If you are not satisfied with your current position in life, flush out the excuses and victim's mentality. That mentality causes you to believe that you are powerless and helpless, unable to change your situation. You may have been using that alibi to feel comfortable and content on your couch.

When the situation is beyond our control, we decide how we respond to it. There is always an unseen benefit behind every dark cloud. Focus on finding the solutions rather than dwelling on your seemingly impossible problems. You don't pay your bills by thinking too much about how many there are, but by increasing your income to have enough to pay those bills. Expand on your energy to generate solutions, and create the environment to obtain more. The universe is here to support you.

Choosing a life of growth is not the same as growing physically from age 1 to 20. Do you remember your early school years where you learned a, b, c, or 1+1=2?

Progressively, as you moved to higher grades and college, things started changing. It was no longer about regular math, but many other subjects, some easier than others. Your knowledge level increases anytime you move to a different class or acquire new information. Gail Sheehy stated, "If we don't change, we don't grow. If we don't grow, we are not really living". Would you rather be comfortable in 12th grade and be settled because you hear your friends say that things get harder in college? Growth demands that you expand your limits by breaking the walls of your comfort zone and venture into other realms where you can learn and develop what you have already acquired and then explore new dimensions. Growth implies change.

Make the choice to grow because your dreams and goals are bigger than the status quo. The only way you will improve the quality of your life is to continue growing and better yourself.

Growth is often uncomfortable and does not happen when you are in a stale mode. As Bob Riggs perfectly said, "Many of us have established a comfort zone in our lives. We are coasting along, taking the path of least resistance, and just getting by. This is a very common and understandable attitude. We have all worked hard to get to where we are, and it may seem a good place to be. The problem with this is that once we stop reaching, stretching, seeking, and risking, we stop growing. The comfort zone frame of mind is settling for what we are today. That may be fine today, but without continuous growth, we remain in our strict size. If you're in a comfort zone, beware – the danger of a comfort zone is that it doesn't hurt, and it may even feel good."

Change your lifestyle, your situation, and make the steps toward your goals through personal growth. If you want to feel more included in some groups, grow your people skills; make yourself the subject of your growth. Do not let any day go by without learning something new. If you are not fond of reading, make it a goal to pick a book and read at least one page a day until it becomes a habit to read a book a week or a day. Change calls for stepping into the unknown and taking risks. Success is not just a fruit you pluck from a tree in a garden. Even if it is so, are you the one who planted the tree? Do you want to wait another day to start your walk toward growth and self-improvement? The choice is yours.

Your growth will not happen automatically. Your age does not define your level of maturity and choosing to grow is your responsibility. Make it an urgent matter by starting today.

Accepting challenges also produces growth and progress. It toughens people up so they can handle change, overcome risk resistance, and stretch themselves to adapt to new realities. Moreover, growth attracts capable friends who challenge one another to achieve higher objectives.

Successful people pivot to other approaches to ensure long-term growth. Then they invest in the strategic innovation to support and increase this growth. Do not view your personal development as a cost, but as an investment in yourself that will pay off in your growth.

Are you teachable? Can you take off your ego hat, empty your cup or make it half-full to add more knowledge?

However successful you are today, do not settle for it. Les Brown asserted, "You have got to be hungry." Do not enjoy your comfort zone too long and do not allow your current success to hold you still. There is more greatness in you that the world needs.

# CHOOSE YOUR FRIENDS

*"Choose your friends with caution; plan your future with purpose and frame your life with faith."* — Thomas S. Monson

Assess your surrounding and carefully choose the people you call 'friends.' Are they the type of persons you want to be and become? Are you just a follower or a student of life? What qualities do your friends have? How did they become your friends?

Looking at your friends often tells you a lot about what you value in people. Now think about a specific close friend. What does she/he do that makes you proud of her/him? An adage says, "A man is known by the company he keeps." Therefore, it is important for your well-being to be a great friend to someone and to have a group of people supporting you. Nevertheless, you must be careful about those with whom you spend a lot of time. People have the propensity to emulate the habits and adopt the interests and opinions of their close friends. As a result, they inadvertently embrace the values they profess.

Choose to have friends you can rely on and who can participate in your growth. Be loyal to your friends and help develop a sense of trust, non-judgment and sensitivity to their feelings, and mainly no put-downs.

I befriended Isaac Vanstory, a talented gentleman who unknowingly taught me the importance of going above and beyond for someone. My car had broken down, and I was in the process of buying another one. While I was waiting for my agent to find me another car, Isaac would take me to work and pick me in the evening. On the weekends, he took me places and literally refused to let me fuel his car. He had given me a ride for two consecutive weeks. He always said, "Don't worry about it. I got you. This is what a friend does for a friend." Isaac does not hesitate to be up front with me whenever my behavior does not match my blueprints. Throughout his actions, I have developed a higher sense of humility, kindness, and availability for others.

Choose to surround yourself with people who can add values to your life for betterment. Get close to those who are more knowledgeable in different areas so you can learn from them. Associate with experienced people who can counsel you instead of just giving you their opinions. Identify and stay away from people whose behaviors and actions are contrary to your values. Remember, sometimes your closest friends can become your closest enemies. Observe their way of life, their sincerity, and sense of comradery. Give your unconditional support to them and choose people who love you out of choice not out of compulsion and benefits.

Choose to stay away from people who have the tendency to control your life and dictate the course of it. Give the best of yourself to them as you receive what they have to offer.

## CHOOSE TO BE GRITTY

*"Everyone can rise above their circumstances and achieve success if they are dedicated to and passionate about what they do."* —
*Nelson Mandela*

Be passionate about your life. After conducting over one hundred interviews, I have discovered that most successful people choose to live passionately in all areas of their life. They feel more energetic and happy.

The choice of passion and perseverance helps you to live in agreement with your values and goals. Passion moves you to invest as much time and energy as necessary to achieve your goals. Like my mentor, Dr. Jermaine M. Davis always says, "Be gritty. Live with passion and persevere in achieving your goals."

Be prepared to face obstacles, to fall and get up. Whenever the going gets tough, toughen yourself up and keep on progressing. Do not fall into the victim mindset or allow excuses to slow you down and stop you.

Be crystal clear about your passion and persevere till you materialize it. Think about the impact you want to make and the purpose behind your passion. That passion will sustain your walk toward your success. Keep on learning, and put your best forward.

Think about where you want to be and immerse yourself with those who have similar goals. Reinforce your willpower by always visiting the reason for achieving your goals and their importance to you.

## CHOOSE TO LIVE WITH GRATITUDE

*"Nothing new can come into your life unless you open yourself up to being grateful."* — Dr. Michael Beckwith

Gratitude flows from the ability to be thankful. Gratitude is a way of life. It involves making a conscious decision to focus on life's blessings rather than its shortcomings. Every moment of our life is full of opportunities to fill our mind with deep feelings of thankfulness and appreciation. When we choose to live with gratitude, we learn to live in a state of grace and humility.

> What are you grateful for? Do you take your life or your possessions for granted?
>
> Do you ask yourself why you wake up in the morning and feel alive?
>
> Do you take a minute to look through the window, glance at the sun on the horizon, breathe the fresh air, and feel the morning dew?
>
> What do you first think about in the morning when you wake up?
>
> What do you allow your mind to focus on when waking up?

Nothing new can come into your life unless you are grateful for what you already have. Iyanla Vanzant said "We think we have to do something to be grateful or something has to be done in order for us to be grateful, when gratitude is a state of mind."

> Every day, we wake up willingly or unwilling to face different opportunities, to learn, grow, and expand our ability to live and love. Life is so fragile, yet precious.
>
> An attitude of gratitude causes us to rise above negative emotions such as fear, condemnation, greed, jealousy, and failure. With gratitude, acknowledge and appreciate your life and its blessings. With gratitude, we thank the universe for welcoming us into this life. Cultivate the habit of being grateful even in the toughest moments of your life.
>
> Do not let the quest for success and happiness define your gratitude rather, let your gratitude be the foundation for your success and happiness. As Maya Angelou said, "Let gratitude be the pillow upon which you kneel to say your nightly prayer." Let gratitude be at the core of everything you are experiencing in your life. Be grateful.

People pray more than usual when they are encountering challenges or obstacles in life. They seem more devoted and faithful to call on the universe for help and to fortify themselves in those moments of adversity, illness, pain, or suffering.

How would you feel if someone calls you only when he/she is in need? It is only when they need your service, support, money or presence that their number shows up on your telephone screen. They have never called you to extend a simple two second greetings: 'I'm just calling to say, Good morning, evening or night; I am calling to see how you are feeling today and if there is any way I can be helpful to you.'

When is the last time you have called someone, and told them how grateful you are to have them in your life?

Do not wait until the moment of need to show gratitude.

Gratitude is gold. It can take you from feeling sorry about yourself to feeling great and happy. New scientific research reveals that doing a daily gratitude exercise will make you feel happier, more self-disciplined, more goal-oriented, and even physically healthier. Gratitude frees people from emotional pain and fear. It is not enough to think about gratitude but you have to feel it in your emotions, and then express that gratitude beyond yourself toward others. Execute your daily gratitude exercise. [*Emote – Extend – Exercise*]

---

*Choose to live with gratitude unconditionally and selflessly because "Gratitude is not only the greatest of virtues, but the parent of all the others"* — *Cicero*

---

One of my friends always calls me 'crazy' whenever I pass my hands on my car and simply say, "Thank you, I am grateful for your strength, your obedience and for carrying me to my destinations and bringing me back."

Live with gratitude because from it is born the strength to face life with a smile.

Choose to live with gratitude because our giving becomes our receiving; our compassion becomes our emotion when we are with others.

Beware not to confuse gratitude with indebtedness which only buys someone's loyalty. Indebtedness is seeking to repay a benefactor. It is more about returning something to someone rather than giving. Gratitude embodies a purer feeling, an unselfish desire that has no expectations for reward, repayment, or debt. The choice of gratitude creates a higher frequency where the energy we get out of our thoughts and actions uses the law of attraction to bring the energy back from the universe. Grateful actions toward others result in deserving greater gratitude.

# CHOOSE RESILIENCE

On September 2, 2013, Diana Nyad, a 64-year-old woman swam across the ocean from Havana, Cuba to Key West, Florida. It took her 53 hours to cover 110 miles. She swam longer than I worked at my job in a week. I cannot run 10 miles without feeling my heart drop. She swam without the protection of a shark cage.

When Nyad tried the first time, she was 29 years old. The wind was so strong that she couldn't make enough progress. The second time, she had an asthma attack and had to stop. The third time, she suffered serious jellyfish stings. The fourth time, she encountered a storm that was too dangerous for her to continue.

The fifth time, she started on August 31st and finished on September 2nd. But this time, she had done several things that she hadn't done before. The forecast was in her favor because the wind would be blowing in the direction of her destination. She also had a special swimming gear on that protected her against the stings of the jellyfish. After 53 hours, she completed what no one else has ever done. The 64-year-old Nyad swam up to the beach just before 2 pm on Saturday, September 2nd.

She said to people, "I have three messages: One, never ever give up. Two, you are never too old to chase your dream. Three, it looks like a solitary sport, but it is a team." During her interview, she said, "I think that a lot of people in our country have gotten depressed, pinned in, pinned down with living their lives the way they don't want."

Are you living your life the way you don't want?

Diana Nyad was eight years old when she first dreamed about swimming across the Straits of Florida when she was on a trip to Cuba with her parents in the 1950s.

While the final destination may give you a sense of satisfaction, the journey is what gives the excitement and fulfillment. The preparation and the journey are what lies in the dash of your life - between the day you were born and the day you depart-. Your life accomplishments do not happen instantaneously. They are part of your journey. It takes decisions and focus on accomplishing something. In our society, most people want everything to happen overnight, right now. We want to lose weight now; we want to achieve financial freedom right now; we want to be healthy now.

People who expect an overnight success are sure to become frustrated after one failure. They say, "I have been trying for so long, but it is not happening. It is not meant for me." We hear it all the time.

It took Nyad 56 years to finally achieve her goal. Besides the most valuable lesson is when she said "…talking to you about the journey is worth everything. It is." Fulfill your dreams and goals as long as you have breath in your lungs. "You tell me what your dreams are. What are you chasing that seems impossible? Name it," Nyad asserted. There will be times where we feel like going back to the conformity of our life.

That is the exact moment when we should hold on tight and learn all we can.

Some people develop a culture of abdication and giving up becomes the main chorus of every song:

I do not like my job, I quit.

My boss made me mad, I quit.

My coworkers snitched on me, I quit.

This is too difficult, I quit.

I do not like my shape, I quit.

My husband/wife doesn't love me anymore, I quit.

My kids do not listen to me, I quit.

My business is not growing, I quit.

I think it is too hard to be successful, I quit.

As a matter of fact, I quit, I quit, and I quit.

So, do you quit too, just in a blink of an eye? Do you? Are you a pitiful quitter?

"It is not my fault!" Oh, really? Is that the best answer you can give?

"Never quit. It is the easiest cop-out in the world. Set a goal and do not quit until you attain it. When you do attain it, set another goal, and do not quit until you reach it. Never quit." Bear Bryant.

Habibo Haji, a young lady who lives in Rochester, MN, was raised as a shepherd girl and a nomad at the early age of 5, herding her family cows and facing dangers by herself everyday while in the wilderness in her home country Somalia. She then, moved to the largest refugee camp in Kenya for three years facing malicious attacks from insurgents. Fortunately, at the age of 16, she was selected to immigrate to the United States. She did not speak a word of English; she had no family and no money. She could have simply settled into the welfare system but she chose otherwise.

Habibo made the decision to enroll in school, learn to speak, read and write English, graduated from Augsburg College and is now a Registered Nurse at the Mayo Clinic. When I asked her how she did it, she responded "We are the drivers of our own destiny. I could have waited for someone to make a miracle happen in my life which means I would wait until I die, but I decided to make my own miracles. I decided that it is up to me to shape my destiny and pave the way for my children. I had to break the cycle of poverty, period."

Her book *Conquering the Odds, The Journey of a Shepherd Girl* relates her experiences, hardships, fears and her determination and resilience to accomplish that which she desires to become.

Successful people are masters of both persistence and quitting. When they quit, they completely detach from their previous goals and devote themselves to pursuing new ones.

Instead of quitting for the heck of it, or because you are encountering some difficulties, you can choose a healthy quitting. It consists of stopping a course of action in a thoughtful, deliberate manner to pursue a new plan, more fitting for your goals. It does not mean you stop moving towards your goals. As you acquire new knowledge, information, and skills, you may discover a need to adjust your path.

> *"If you live long enough, you'll make mistakes. But if you learn from them, you'll be a better person. It's how you handle adversity, not how it affects you. The main thing is never quit, never quit, never quit."* — *William J. Clinton*

It is important to learn how to be resilient and face the seasons of your life. You are not the only one going through adversity and challenges. We all endure roadblocks, but the most successful individuals are those who show more resilience and continue their path. Before you throw in the towel and walk away from your goals, consider what your parents went through, so you can be born and live today.

Do not hold onto things you consciously know are keeping you from moving toward your objectives. Those things may be your personal lack of transparency, sincerity, honesty, or lies, laziness, procrastination and fear. Face them and let go of the burden that has ensnared you for so long. Embrace integrity, build a new personality, make some swift shifts, and put the wheel of your life on the road to accomplishments. Run the race with endurance, perseverance, and resiliency. Make the journey to your dreams and goals an exciting one.

## CHOOSE TO LIVE BY FAITH

> *"It is the lack of faith that makes people afraid of meeting challenges."* — *Muhammad Ali*

First, to thyself be faithful because it starts with you.

Do you have faith in yourself and your ability to achieve your goals?

Do you live by faith? It is not if I can see it, I believe it; instead, by faith "If I believe it, I can see it."

Do not neglect your inner spiritual values while pursuing your life goals. Spiritual and emotional traits like determination, discipline, happiness, courage, wisdom, and focus emanate from the mind. The inner life is the driving force that spurs and shepherds people. Your inner disciplines such as meditation, prayer, reflection, and concentration for the mind and spirit is just as important as outer disciplines such as hygiene and good food.

Thoughts govern actions, thus we should develop positive and constructive thought patterns. Healthy thinking, letting go of emotional burdens and forgiving those who may have hurt us in the past, help people overcome their past adversities.

Faith is not the power to succeed, but rather the guidance toward what you want to achieve. Your faith is limited by your capacity to believe. To develop faith with the end of attaining a goal, you must continuously repeat what you wish to come true.

Developing faith is vital because, by it, you can translate your thoughts into reality. Anything given to the subconscious mind with faith and positive emotions will meet with success because thoughts attract other similar or related thoughts.

We become more appreciative of the ups of life when we are experiencing the downs. During those breakdowns, we realize that we need another power, a greater power, to strengthen us to overcome obstacles. Some people call for a miracle to occur and save them. Consequently, it is in those down moments that we call upon God.

Faith is not something you desire or wish. Faith is not pretending that something is true when it is not. Faith is not a feeling.

Faith is not negotiating with God saying, "If God does this to me, I will serve Him forever."

Faith is a way of seeing, looking at the world. As Marianne Williamson said, "To trust in the force that moves the universe is faith. Faith is not blind; it is visionary. Faith is believing that the universe is on our side, and that the universe knows what it's doing."

You can achieve anything if you have faith. Whether you are religious or spiritual, ask for divine guidance in finding the solution. If you are not religious or spiritual, believe in yourself and the infinite Universe to help you find the solution. Developing this attitude of faith will support your efforts toward what you want to achieve. This catalyst makes the greater mind activate and go to work in your life.

Anthony Lewis, a man of faith, has affected my life in so many ways. I can call him anytime, and he is always available, not only to listen to me but not to judge me. We both love good food, and during one of our dinners, Pastor Lewis shared with me the importance of faith.

He told me about his personal life when he was going through some tribulations until the day he decided to change his lifestyle. From a people pleaser to finding his identity, Anthony searched for his values and said that his deeper inspiration to change comes from the Christ in him, his love for God. When he lost his mother, he asked God to help him get out of his habits of smoking, drinking and associating with people who do not have the impact he wanted. And the Lord answered his prayers.

He decided to move to Minnesota where he lives around people who counsel him and want the best for him. He put himself in an environment that shapes his integrity and authenticity. With faith in himself and ultimately in God, Anthony took action toward his goals and aspirations.

His life changed when he found the strength to overcome his obstacles; and in the face of temptation, he casts away the thoughts that are trying to invade his mind and drag him back to his old life.

As he said, "Be who you are, don't paint a picture that does not reflect your identity, for the truth holds the course. Live with transparency and give to people the gift of who you are."

Today Anthony Lewis has two beautiful daughters, and he and his wife Kerry are Pastors. They happily serve the community.

There is an unlimited power within you, but you must decide to utilize it. You must develop an attitude of faith, an attitude of confident expectation that all will be well. Develop your faith; have faith in yourself, and in your ability to create your future. Have faith in people. Help them without expecting a reward, and help them to believe in themselves.

## CHOOSE SELF-DISCIPLINE

*"Discipline determines your destiny, not desire, but self-discipline."*
— *Charles Stanley*

Do you have any demanding goal that requires discipline?

I can eat French fries and omelet all day. I enjoy fried meat and fish. Whenever I go out with friends, no matter what dish I pick, I always add French fries on the side. On a Friday evening, I invited few friends to my apartment and cooked a delicious dinner with fried chicken, fish, and shrimp. Jesse Pulley, a good friend of mine, declined the food and only ate the biscuits. I felt offended and asked him why he did not want to try the fish, shrimp, or chicken.

"No offense intended, do you allow me to share something with you?" Jesse asked.

"Sure, I am all ears," I replied.

"You know I work at the hospital, and I see many patients every day. We only have one life, and we want to enjoy that life and eat whatever we desire. Nonetheless, we need to understand that we have to be healthy to enjoy life.

I attended the funeral of a medical doctor last spring. Her husband, who was also a doctor, shared their story during his eulogy. He said that the cause of his wife's death was heart failure due to her weight. True, his wife looked obese, but she was an excellent surgical doctor. As a doctor, she was conscious of her diet, but always said, "I will eat anything I want as long as I am alive." That was her motto. She did not want to take any advice from her husband and usually said "This is my last time eating cookies," yet five minutes later she will say the same thing again and enjoy her cookies.

In her final moments, she confessed to her husband about her lack of self-discipline and rejection of the advice he had given about her nutrition. She expressed a deep regret, and in tears, she took her last breath. Her husband was so devastated, left with two children. He said in his eulogy that every food is good but the excess of it is the source of many health issues. Therefore, Wisdom, I have known you for many years, and I notice you eat a lot of fried food and cook with a lot of oil. That may increase your cholesterol level. I apologize if I offend you," Jesse finally said.

I paused for a moment and thanked him for the information he shared. Two weeks later, I went to the doctor for my annual checkup, and it revealed that my cholesterol level went from 199 mg/dl to 301 mg/dl. As a result, I was put on medication. I did not think twice before controlling my diet. I do still eat fried food, but in a small quantity and only once a month.

The amazing part of our life is that we know what to do, yet we do not take it upon ourselves to do what is necessary to change. Jim Rohn said, "Your life does not get better by chance; it gets better by change."

Self-discipline is not something we like. People do not like being told what to do or not to do. We like to claim our freedom. With self-discipline, you can put your strategy in place and act toward your goals.

Self-discipline is doing what you have to do when you do not feel like it. People practice discipline when they wake up in the morning and go to work for someone else, but they are unable to apply the same discipline to reach their personal goals and success. Therefore, do not blame anyone, your parents, or your cats and dogs. While looking in the mirror, answer this question: Are you self-disciplined?

On another hand, are you waiting for your friend to work out in your stead, so you can magically lose weight? Are you waiting for your friend to study hard, so you pass your exam?

Nobody achieves and sustains success without self-discipline. No matter how gifted or talented you are, you cannot reach your full potential without being disciplined. It includes understanding the benefits of doing what is right, rather than what is convenient.

If you wish to be successful, study success; do not leave anything to chance. You may not be able to do all you find out but you should find out all you can do. Discipline your mind and thoughts regardless of the adversity even when the going gets hard. Exercise self-discipline over all your emotions: love, hate, fear. We live in a world where people want instant gratification. Do not expect any accomplishments without preceding them with some demanding actions.

Things do not come easily as we want. The Chinese bamboo tree takes five years to break through the seed, but you have to fertilize it, water it consistently; and suddenly after five years, the bamboo tree starts growing and reaches 90 feet tall within six weeks. The question is: does it grow 90 feet in 6 weeks or 5 years?

Self-discipline helps to develop character, and it plays a significant role in the actualization of your dreams, visions, and goals.

Without a clear goal and a plan to achieve it, most people are distracted and lose focus indicating the crucial need for self-discipline. It is the key to self-esteem, self-respect, and personal pride. The development of self-discipline is a guarantee that you will overcome the obstacles and create a better life for yourself and others. Become more of an action-oriented person and think about your next step because any decision is better than no decision. Do not be like someone who sets goals, reads them every day, and expects them to happen without action and discipline. Do you get paid at work just for showing up or for the value you bring to the company?

Darren Hardy in his book *The Compound Effect* said "A daily routine built on good habits and disciplines separates the most successful among us from everyone else. A routine is exceptionally powerful."

Practice these steps

- Think on paper. Before taking action, list the things you must do to solve the problem and get through the crunch. The simplest or most direct solution is often the best one.

- Make a list. You may make a daily list of things to accomplish. The top seven items should be numbered and organized by priority, then accomplished in that order. Self-discipline cannot be a one-time achievement; it should become a way of life. Successful people develop systems and routines that help them practice self-discipline for long-term growth and success.

- Challenge and eliminate any tendency to make excuses. Self-disciplined people learn to postpone rewards until they have reached their goals. They stay focused on the results they want to achieve instead of the difficulty of the work needed to achieve them.

People are not born with self-discipline; they hone it and learn to apply it. The more they use self-discipline, the more effective they become. Self-discipline is not an object or appliance that you can casually turn on and off at will. The achievement of a goal requires a consistent walk.

Be disciplined at measuring, monitoring, and benchmarking your activities, your progress, and your actions, all of which are fundamental practices used to assess performance and identify opportunities for continuous growth towards your success.

Assuming that your goal is to improve your health and lose a certain amount of weight in precisely 90 days, what actions are you taking? Will you find excuses and wait until the 60th day to start eating healthy and working out?

How many people make New Year's resolutions and maintain them for 90 days, six months, or a year. Very, very few. You cannot attain the end in one day. The results manifest through the principle that you can reap huge rewards from a series of small, smart activities that produce a compound effect. Success also comes from self-discipline not just from desire only.

If you can't discipline yourself, don't waste your time setting goals because you won't accomplish anything other than living with excuses and blaming your parents, the nature, even your dog, and cat.

## CHOOSE TO DANCE WITH YOUR EXCUSES

*"If you want to do something, you'll find a way. If you don't, you'll find an excuse."* — *Jim Rhon*

"I am sorry, I can't. I am a very busy person, and I don't have time. I have a lot going on right now. Give me few months."

How many times have people used those phrases? Some did it legitimately, but others use them to escape from doing something. Mostly, these lies appear so blatantly that you have to laugh inwardly when you hear people's excuses.

What are your excuses for not doing what you need to do?

Why are you using those excuses?

Is it because of the weather? Do you mean, because it is raining or snowing today you will not step out to meet the clients? Is that why you will not get out of your bed and work on your assignments, your dream projects? Really? Can you find the difference between reasons and excuses?

You don't have to put a frown on your face. I am just asking.

---

*"Blaming is just another sorry excuse, and making excuses is the first step towards failure"* — *Suman Rai*

---

How many times have people used the conjunction "if" when giving their excuses? Countless times. "If I had a car, I would get a better job. If I were married, I would be happy! Or, if I hadn't married her/him, I would be happier."

James Robertson, 56, a Detroit man, used to walk eight hours to get to his $10.55/hour job as a plastic-molding operator. That routine began when his car broke down in 2005, and the bus service was cut back. By car, it would only be a 20-minute drive. Robertson leaves his house around 8 a.m. to arrive at work ahead of his 2 p.m. shift, which ends at 10 p.m. He catches the last bus toward Detroit at 1 a.m. and does not get home until 4 a.m. His supervisor said James has never been late for the past ten years, and he walked 21 miles every day to work. When he got off work, he only had few hours of sleep and was right back on the road facing the weather until he got to work.

In March 2015, James made the headlines and was appraised with a new car and $350,000. If someone had told him it would take him ten years to own a car, he would not have believed it. If they told him that one day he would walk 21 miles every day to work and make ends meet, he would not believe it. When interviewed, James said he had no excuses to stay home.

Most of the time, when people are coming up with excuses, they use the negative of verbs *cannot*, *will not*, or *do not*. They point to something other than themselves as the cause of their problems and miseries.

Do you make excuses and blame others when something goes awry? The will to succeed does not necessarily guarantee your success. It takes an attitude of resolute vision and actions that flush any excuses coming your way.

Instead of making excuses not to do something, won't it be simpler to make excuses to do things aligned with your goals? If you are so good at inventing excuses not to work out, why not become an expert at finding excuses to go to the gym? You must use self-discipline to resist the lure of excuses. You can turn the negative excuses that keep you in your comfort zone into more positive ones that encourage you to stay the course toward your goals and success. Separate legitimate reasons from excuses.

Practice this faithfully. If you can make excuses not to read a book today, or study, it means you can also make different excuses to help you read a book or attend seminars for your personal growth. It is a simple exercise to shift your paradigm from the negative excuses to more positive ones. Remember this: excuses will always be there for you, but opportunity will not. Once you break the negative excuses mindset, opportunities will flock to you. If your goals are important to you, you will find the excuses to grow. George W. Carver said, "99% of failures come from people who have the habit of making excuses." If you want to succeed, stop saying, "*I can't.*" "*I won't.*" "I might." "*I'll try.*" "*Maybe.*" "*Later.*" or "*Tomorrow*" and start saying, "I am doing it NOW."

# CHOOSE TO BE HAPPY

*"I simply choose to be happy and live my life to the fullness." —*

*Wisdom Primus*

How do you define happiness? How do you know you are happy? Do you premise your happiness on something you are expecting? Are you happy because you make it second nature to be happy for no apparent reason? Are you brightening someone's day wherever you go?

We all want to be happy. We want to live a happy life but for many of us, happiness is an elusive, fleeting state that we can capture only for a brief moment before it vanishes. As human beings, majority of our forward action is driven by the pursuit of happiness. People link everything they are looking for -love, social life, - to being happy. Most of the time, we relate our happiness to possessions: 'when I have a new car, I will be happy.' Few months after you buy that car, the excitement and happiness fade away. The pursuit of better jobs, higher status, and more wealth – the root of everything we are chasing is happiness. However, how long does that form of happiness last? Do you find yourself being happy all the time? When a reason determines the condition for our happiness, it can become the source of our misery. This certainly does not mean that everything we chase will bring us happiness. In fact, a big part of our struggle in life is figuring out what makes us really and deeply happy, and more importantly, what makes us consistently happy.

In the book, *What Happy People Know*, the authors stated that, "Happiness isn't the art of building a trouble-free life. It's the art of responding well when trouble strikes."

Life is too short to live negatively and let daily challenges crush our inner happiness. Do not compare your situation with anyone else's. You have everything you need to live happily. You may not be in the home of your dreams, or have the exact job you would like to have but it certainly does not mean you cannot be happy. It is good to have goals beyond our present circumstances, but we cannot let the challenges of life frustrate us to become unhappy and miserable. How will you feel if you have an inexhaustible happiness that flows in you constantly?

Happiness in its essence is not a mood or an emotional state. It is a way of life composed of gratitude, optimism, love, compassion, or other ingredients. Beware of the quest for happiness; it may lead you to fall in its usual lure. When you define your happiness by what you possess, you are making happiness a commodity to purchase. It may serve you for a short time but is that the type of happiness you have longed to have? Look back in your life. Have you had a day where you were happy for no particular reason? Do you remember being happy because you had an inner peace? What feelings did you have during that day? You woke up, and all you saw in the mirror was happiness. Have you ever experienced that unexplained happiness where you were grateful for everything in life? That is the actual happiness you need to seek every day. It will not come to you suddenly because you want it.

Are you able to smile at anyone you come across even though, they do not return the favor? Do you give with a kind heart without necessarily expecting something in return? Start working on being appreciative of things in your life. Appreciation is the purest form of love. It helps combat fear and releases the deepest happiness in you. Identify your strengths and focus on maximizing them instead of dwelling on your weaknesses, which only reinforces your challenges. During some job interviews, you may be required to name your weaknesses. Thus, people think that focusing on their weakness will enable them to turn it into strength. Rather, discover your inner strength and amplify it. For instance, take the strength finder test and enhance your abilities and talents.

## CHOOSE YOUR LANGUAGE

*"Let no corrupt communication proceed out of your mouth, but that which is good to the use of edifying, that it may minister grace unto the hearers."– Ephesians 4:29 (KJV)*

"I wish someone else hurts you the way you have done to me. I can't stand you. You are obnoxious, dangerous, horrible, stupid ... You are nothing but a pig." Luther angrily said to his girlfriend.

Take a toothpaste tube; squeeze it until all the paste is out. Now put the paste back in the tube. Can you? Even if you can do it, how long will it take you? That's what happens when you say words to hurt another person. You can't take those words back. They are like arrows piercing a tree. The wounds created by the arrows will always leave a scar after they heal. Soon afterward, Luther's anger dissipated. He ran to his girlfriend and apologized, "I am so sorry, baby. I was angry at you and didn't mean what I said earlier. Will you forgive me? I am really sorry." The girlfriend looked at him and burst into tears.

*"Language is the bridge between the creative and uncreative worlds. We humans use language as the vehicle to deliver content, however we are mostly unaware that the context is being delivered as well."*

*– Roberto Fonts, C.E.O. Dialog-One*

Language is used to express our thoughts and feelings. It is used to express ourselves. We must harness our language if we are to be successful in its usage. Just like the example of the toothpaste, you can't take those words back after you speak them. No apology is powerful enough to soothe and wipe out the pain they caused to others. Spoken words are a reflection of our thoughts, and an expression of our feelings.

My friend Luther may have thought he was directing those words toward his girlfriend, but it was actually toward himself. How? Who is the source of those words? Those spoken words emanate from him, his inside. And what is inside of you is part of you. He may think he is describing his girlfriend, but he is in fact pointing to what is inside him. He may not know it. We have to be careful about the type of thoughts we allow into our mind. Because the language that stems from those thoughts are as powerful as water and wind.

Haven't you seen the incredible power of ocean waves or a huge waterfall? What you allow inside, will shape who you are. And the more you use those words; you will likely attract people with the same language. Control your thoughts; control what goes inside you. As a result, your words will be more productive and constructive than destructive. If the image projected by a mirror is your own, what makes you think your spoken words reflect another person's? You are the one revealed by your words.

In your process to become successful, use the power of the spoken word to call for what you want instead of what you don't want. We live in a universe that listens to us. Change the direction of your life; begin to speak what you want over your life.

Dr. Masaru Emoto discovered that when directing words and thoughts to water, those words with positive energy formed clear crystal snowflakes when that water is frozen. But when negative words and thoughts are directed to water, the snowflakes appear as misshapen blobs when water is frozen. Our body is 80% water thus the words you speak produce an effect that corresponds to the meaning of those words. Use your thoughts and your words wisely to affirm positive happenings in your life and those around you. When you face adversity caused by friends or situations, do not take offense. When you pay close attention to their words, you will notice that they are saying the negative qualities they possess. Through the law of mirror, people can only reflect what they are. Use the power of the spoken words to create, to build, to erect, to blossom and above all, to love. Words are just words. How we use them or associate with them, create the impact.

Because the words we speak either aloud, or in the privacy of our mind, embody our intentions; they are a carrier of ourselves, our energy. We can choose to pass on negativity or positivity in our speech. Our words do matter. They are powerful. Change your thoughts and your words and attract the being you want to be. Start by doing these six things:

1. *Be genuine*

Give sincere compliments to yourself and people around you. Wherever you see hatred, send thoughts of love. Show your appreciation and gratitude to people around you. Give praise without attachment. Say "thank you."

2. *Think and speak aloud*

Settle in and enjoy yourself. Have positive, blessing, and healing thoughts and words to yourself and others.

3. *Practice positive self-talk*

As you go about your daily activities, be conscious of how you are talking to yourself in your mind. Practice accepting compliments graciously. Be accurate with your thoughts and words. Guard your mind against thoughts that do not produce positive results. Find aspects of your behavior you can genuinely positively praise. Make a list of positive power words or phrases:

| Abundant | Positive |
| Active | Confident |

| | |
|---|---|
| Considerate | Attractive |
| Engaging | Passionate |
| Exceptional | Friendly |
| Radiant | Harmonious |

Enrich your vocabulary with words that are meaningful to you based on what you want in your life. Write them down and post them on your mirror, wherever you can see them and say them out loud.

4. *Responding instead of reacting.*

To react is to speak without thought or to blurt. To respond implies conscious thought. In responding, we choose our words. Think before you speak. Weigh your words and speak wisely.

5. *Learn to say and receive "I forgive you."*

If we accept or give a sincere apology, the sting of the offense is removed. Sometimes we carry blame, guilt, or anxiety for years because we assume the damage caused by our actions lives on. If we'd been told we were forgiven, the burden should have been released. Like "I'm Sorry", "I forgive you" is incredibly powerful.

6. *Read books.*

Make it a habit of enriching your vocabulary through reading. The more words you have, the more precisely you can express yourself.

## CHOOSE TO BE NICE

*"There is nothing more beautiful than someone who goes out of their way to make life beautiful for others." – Mandy Hale*

How many times have you been at a store and seen items on the floor? Sometimes you see people drop items from the shelves, and they are so lazy to put them back. When you ask them to do it, their favorite answer is, "I am not paid to do it," or "I don't work here."

What does it cost you to keep the door open for a stranger when you walk in a store or offer to help someone? Nothing! It costs nothing to be nice. It calls for others to do the same thing for you when you expect it the least. Being kind to one another is uniquely human. It does not require a college degree or an exceptional talent and skill.

It was late at night on an icy road when I witnessed a car swerving and ending up in the ditch. Though I was in a rush to get home, I decided to stop and moved to offer assistance. As I was approaching them to confirm their welfare, the driver yelled and ordered me not to get close, or he would shoot me. Another person in the car said, "Seriously? The guy is offering to help us, and you want to shoot him? It is snowing, and we do not know how long the police will take to get here? Sir, we need help," the lady screamed.

The engine of their car died, and we were in a cold Minnesota winter breeze. I offered to let them sit in my car. There were four people, the couple, and their daughters and despite the appreciation from his wife and children, the husband kept his hand on the pistol in his pocket. I was at first so frightened at the sight of the gun. When the assistance came, I took off and continued my way.

---

*"...You're not going to be the tallest, fastest, prettiest, the best track runner, but you can be the nicest human being that someone has ever met in their life. And I just want to leave the legacy that being nice is a true treasure."* — *George Foreman*

---

The following day, on my way back from work, I saw a lady on highway I-35N, leaving her car alongside the road and walking. I exited and came back to help. Her car had also broken down, and her cell phone's battery was dead. I let her use my phone, and she called her husband. I offered to drop her wherever her husband was. Upon our arrival, we were both shocked to see each other. The husband was the mail carrier at my workplace! He broke into tears of joy.

Being nice and kind is the simplest thing to do. Choose to be helpful and show gratitude towards others.

## CHOOSE TO HAVE FUN

*"People rarely succeed unless they have fun in what they are doing"*— Dale Carnegie

Having fun does not mean getting drunk and wasted or partying until dawn. Having fun lies in the type of atmosphere you create while you are at work, on the playground, or working on your dreams. Put the stress away by bringing joy and pleasure into your activities. Maybe you like to play music on a piano, guitar, or another instrument, go for it, and play as much as you want. It does not need to be a perfect symphony. As long as you enjoy doing it, do not stop. Take a walk and watch the sunset. If you enjoy baking, make some cakes, cookies and share with people. Break out of the routine.

Your goals are important, but your happiness is crucial. Take a moment and be silly; go on a vacation; do whatever you want without pressure. Go fishing, ice skating, rock climbing, go and visit a fair. Go to a garage sale. Take time to do whatever makes you happy.

Remember something you liked to do when you were younger or something you want to experience. Fill up your car tank and go for a drive in the countryside, by a lake, or anywhere you want.

Don't just focus too much on activities that you lack the ability to relax. Just like Tommy Bolin illustrated, "If you are not having fun, it's not worth doing." Your goals and success are your destinations. More importantly, the path you pave during that process is what makes you a successful person. Build that path with happiness; enjoy every moment you spend working towards your goals.

Be a happy person. Work and fun are not at all exclusive of each other. We need to take a break and have fun to maintain a balance in life.

Have you ever heard someone say, "Work hard, play hard?" Give yourself the time to rejoice and enjoy yourself after an activity. Give yourself a pat on the back for a milestone achieved. Save $10, $20, or $100 and celebrate. Go to the movies, go to a restaurant, and order a special meal. Reward yourself with a gift you know that you deserve. What I am saying is to treat yourself like a king, celebrate yourself at least once a month because you deserve it after putting effort into an activity or achieving a milestone. When you treat yourself, you acknowledge yourself and your hard work. Take a moment and have fun in the pursuit of your success.

Please don't get drunk, drive and hurt someone. That is not fun.

# CONCLUSION

"What we're willing to give up in the pursuit of a dream. Stop kidding yourselves. Go after what you want. There is no sacrifice in success, there are no obstacles. There is nothing between you and the goal. You see, if you succeed on your terms, you don't owe anybody any explanations. But if you fail on their terms, you've got a lot of explaining to do. A man doesn't strive for greatness and embrace mediocrity.

There is no compromise in a dream. Compromise?

It's an excuse for falling short while you lay on your couches, in front of your TVs, with your remote controls, and your glasses of beer watching somebody else run with your dream…Your Dream!

So, do me a favor, don't wake up one morning, when your hair is gray, and the elastic has gone out of your waistline, with shaving cream all over your faces, and you look in that mirror and you ask yourselves 'What the hell have I been doing for the last 30 years? This isn't my life! This isn't where my passion lies!' Do something before that happens!

Don't be afraid of your ambitions. If other people hold you back, you don't want it badly enough and don't tell me you do… because other people don't stop you from dreaming. You stop yourself. You get in your own way! Because you're afraid of what you might become, even if that something is a wonderful, wonderful thing. Thank you"

Danny Aiello, — from the opening monologue in the movie "*The Closer*"—

Wisdom Primus holds a Bachelor and Master's degrees in Social Sciences, Applied Economics and Marketing. He has delivered keynote presentations on positive character traits, how to beat procrastination, develop self-confidence and achieve greatness. Wisdom has spoken at non-profits organizations, colleges, universities and community centers, church, youth groups…

To book Wisdom Primus for your next event,

To learn more about Wisdom's lectures and workshops, go to

www.wisdomprimus.com

www.servewithpassion.com

Or contact him at +1 (612) 223-0300

Printed in Great Britain
by Amazon